...ad Gate aforesaid in the Town

... of Richard Carlec... ...ra...

...ay open to and w... ...ea

Dwellinghouses formerly Hood

James Mantle afterwards of...

Powell, Glazier, and afterwa...

James Kinnersley and Lucy...

...Wall on the South and the...

...erected and built on the yeike...

...West side thereof theretofore in the...

...d also all that part of the sai...

...the same Garden by a Wall an...

...ment Westwardly to the said...

...y open to the said above men...

... of the said Lucy Maria...

...aments and Premises were par...

THE BROAD GATE

THE BROAD GATE

A Ludlow House and its Inhabitants

Valerie Thomas

LEFT FIELD EDITIONS
LUDLOW

First published in 2020 by Left Field Editions
Text © 2020 Valerie Thomas

British Library in Cataloguing Publishing Data:
A catalogue entry for this publication is available from the British Library

ISBN 978 1 5272 6696 4

Left Field Editions
9 Lower Raven Lane, Ludlow SY8 1BL

Printed in Malta by Gutenberg Press

TO KEITH

THE BROAD GATE IN MEDIEVAL TIMES
An impression of the towers by Peter Brears

CONTENTS

ILLUSTRATIONS

1. THE BROAD GATE FROM BROAD STREET
A present-day view of the north front of the house

PREFACE AND ACKNOWLEDGEMENTS

This is the history of a house and its development from a medieval fortified gatehouse in the Ludlow town walls, to a Georgian gentleman's residence and family home. The people who inhabited the Broad Gate for any length of time often came from very large, extended families, but this account is primarily concerned with those who actually lived in the house, or who knew it well. I have concentrated on the four families who were instrumental in the creation of the house: the Steads, the Sprotts, the Kinnersleys and the Lloyds. There is hardly any evidence of them as individuals; no diaries, few letters or accounts until the twentieth century, no memoirs or unvarnished descriptions of them, and few portraits. Wills are often the only indication of character, by revealing which objects or relatives the testator most valued. But wills can be very brief or obscured by legal jargon and formulae, and they can also be misleading. The phrase 'my dearly beloved wife', which features in so many wills, is no guarantee that it was a happy marriage. The stipulation 'for her own use' was a common way of providing for daughters without their husbands' interference, and for getting round the laws of 'coverture'. The absence of one or other possible legatee may not imply rejection; provision may have been made beforehand, as in the case of Evan Lloyd of Weobley and his eldest son. An attempt has therefore been made to set the families in the social and professional context of Ludlow itself, to show what kind of life the inhabitants of the Broad Gate lived, and how they used the house.

As far as possible, material has been drawn from contemporary sources. The punctuation in the quotations has occasionally been modernised, but the spelling has been left as it is. A serious problem in dealing with the families has been their repeated use of the same first names: John in the Stead family; Thomas, Henry, Dorothy, Isabella, Mary and Anne in the Sprott family; and seven Evans among the Lloyds. To clarify this, I have provided family trees, and given capital letters to those who actually lived in the house. I have standardised the spelling of these names. Anne, for instance, often appears as Ann for the same individual, and is occasionally latinised as Anna, but she appears here as Anne throughout.

I have been fortunate to possess the deeds of the Broad Gate, dating from the eighteenth century, and, over the years, have collected pictures and artefacts connected to the house. I have also used photographs of other items. While every effort has been made to establish the whereabouts of the originals, it has not been possible in one or two cases.

I could not have embarked on this book without relying on the previous work of two unrelated Lloyds, both, sadly, no longer with us. David Lloyd was a distinguished local historian of Ludlow. His magisterial doctoral thesis on house ownership in the town, and his research on the houses in Broad Street have been invaluable; notes he provided on the Broad Gate itself have been a crucial starting-point. Michael Lloyd, a descendant of a member of the legal family which came to own the house, put together a family history of the Lloyds which has been indispensable. My great regret is that I did not meet him or his second cousin, Mary Lloyd, who was one of the last Lloyds to live at the Broad Gate, and who was still alive when we arrived. She could have answered so many questions.

I have been greatly helped and encouraged by the Ludlow Historical Research Group, who inherited David Lloyd's archive and papers, and gave me access to them. In particular, I have to thank Rosalind Caird, who transcribed some of the Easter Books, Derek Beattie, who read the text and made helpful suggestions, and, above all, Michael Page, who has been exploring the early building of the town walls and the Broad Gate, and who generously allowed me to use some of his research, particularly in the early chapters. Present members of the Lloyd family, Heather Lloyd and her son, Richard, have taken a keen interest and have supplied me with documents, pictures, photographs, and extra information about the family. Malcolm Pinhorn, who is related to one of the Lloyd wives, gave me a splendid photograph of members of the family, and passed on details of the Leominster branch of the legal practice.

I am indebted to staff at the Hereford Archives and Records Centre and Shropshire Archives, to Maggie Waldman of the Weobley and District Local History Society, and to Ruth Wilford of the Shropshire Family History Society. Sue Hubbard, curator of the Weobley Museum, has been particularly enthusiastic, and has gone the extra mile in transcribing for me the very long and illegible will of Evan Lloyd of Weobley. She and Norman Haynes also managed to identify the house in Weobley lived in by Evan Lloyd and his family, and the farm where he raised cattle.

I am also grateful to the following: Janet Stead for information on the Stead family; George Alderson of the Eardisland History Group for help with the Kinnersleys; Dr David Slater and Bryan Heatley for their work on local canals; Dr Peter Elmer, who has researched medical practitioners in the early eighteenth century; and my grandson, John Gowers, for setting out the family trees so carefully. Neil Guy's knowledge of medieval castles has been invaluable, and my understanding of the Georgian period has been greatly enriched by membership of the local Georgian Group, run for around twenty-five years by the late Julia Ionides. Julia took us on many visits to local houses and beyond, and ran exciting and enlightening weekend courses on all aspects of Georgian life, from ice houses to ballooning.

I owe special thanks to David Burnett, my publisher, for his advice, his encouragement and his fund of imaginative ideas; to Pete MacKenzie who designed the book, and who has been infinitely patient and flexible in response to many demands through many drafts; and to Mark Ansell who came on delightful trips to darkest Shropshire and beyond to take photographs of houses and church monuments. I also owe an enormous debt to Tim Smith who has been so assiduous in discovering out-of-the-way illustrations, like the hitherto unknown George Jones sketch from Rhode Island Museum, and the superb painting of the Ludlow carrier from Basel; and to Peter Brears, who has given expert help in interpreting the kitchen arrangements, and has brought the house to life in his detailed watercolours.

Above all, I thank my husband, Keith, who has been such a support and inspiration for nearly sixty years. Much against his better judgment, he bought the house, but he has enjoyed it with me ever since.

V.T.   *Ludlow, September 2020*

*BROAD STREET, LUDLOW, IN THE 1840s
with the Broad Gate estate highlighted*

2. THE GATEWAY UNDER THE HOUSE
showing the arched rebate which would have held the portcullis

INTRODUCTION

1. THE WALLS AND THE GATES

The first recorded event in the history of the Broad Gate is a murder. In 1272 'Roger de la Haye and Henry le Mon together guarded the gate of the Brodestrete in the town of Ludlow, and, moved by contention, Henry killed Roger'.[1] At the time, they should have been guarding one of the main gates in the town walls against the incursions of the Welsh, but no doubt they were bored, as Welsh attacks on Ludlow took place infrequently if at all, though there was unrest on the border, which was only a few miles away to the west.

Ludlow is not mentioned in *Domesday Book* (1086). It was established by the Lacy family of marcher lords from the manor of Stanton. Like many Norman families in the area at the end of the eleventh century, they built a castle on a nearby hill to defend themselves against the Welsh, but they also went on to develop a planned town in a grid on the southern slopes below. The site was well protected by the steep escarpment to the north, and by the rivers Teme and Corve to the south and west. The church of St Laurence first appears in records in 1199,[2] but the town had been growing in importance since the building of the Castle in 1086, and by the thirteenth century it was felt necessary to build walls around it, originally for defence, but increasingly to reflect civic pride and to give status to its overlord. These were complete, with their gates, by about 1300.

The four main gates to the town were Corve Gate, Galdeford Tower, Old Gate and Broad Gate. There were also three minor 'postern' gates at the Linney, Dinham and Mill Street. In addition, the northern stretch of Corve Street, which was outside the town walls, had its own 'nether' gate. Travellers from Wales would have crossed the Teme at Dinham Bridge and come into the town through Dinham Gate; those coming from Shrewsbury and Chester in the north would have entered via Corve Street and Corve Gate; from London and Worcester they would have come through Galdeford Gate, or followed the Teme to Old Gate; from Hereford in the south they would at first have crossed the river by the ford at Ludford, but when the bridge was built they would have come over the bridge, up Lower Broad Street and through the Broad Gate. Of the seven gates, the Broad Gate is the most complete survivor.

Today, visitors travelling into Ludlow from the south will be impressed by the dramatic twin towers framing the entrance to Broad Street, and those who know Ludlow itself will be familiar with the view from the top of the hill to the castellated house which crosses it. Where there was originally a gated entrance through the wall, flanked by the two towers, there is now a large Gothick house built over that gateway and looking north towards the town itself.

The history of the house is, to a large extent, bound up with the architectural history of Broad Street itself, its present eighteenth-century character and its medieval past. All the main streets in Ludlow command distant views of the countryside, but Broad Street has the added drama of two distinctive buildings which enclose it in a defined space, almost like a long oval piazza. At the top, the street is dominated by the Buttercross, with its classical Georgian elegance. At the bottom are the remains of the medieval fortified gateway, supporting a house that, with its battlements, is an eighteenth-century tribute to the Castle. Broad Street is the street that Sir Nikolaus Pevsner described as 'one of the most memorable streets in England'.[3] Long before, in the early sixteenth century, John Leland, on his tour of the principal towns of England, had remarked that Ludlow was 'well-walled', and that the Broad Gate 'ledyth to Brad Strete, the fayrest part of the towne'.[4]

Nowadays, the Broad Gate divides Broad Street from Lower Broad Street, which is outside the walls, and it requires pedestrians and wheeled traffic to negotiate a tunnel under the house. Although some of the original structure has been hidden by later building, it can be seen from Lower Broad Street to retain most of the towered stone edifice dating from the thirteenth century. The stone is now covered by render, but some of the original arrow slits have been reopened, and the outlines of earlier doors and windows are visible under the arch, as is the groove for lowering the portcullis. For most of its life, the lower parts of the building have had other structures attached to them (see Fig. 5). Chandler's Cottage and the Wheatsheaf Inn were built against the front of the east tower and wrapped around its eastern edge, with cellars adjoining the dungeon in its basement. In these cellars remnants of the stone arches of a bridge over the town ditch are to be found. A seventeenth-century lease to Nicholas Payne, a goldsmith, of what later became Chandler's Cottage (now part of the Wheatsheaf Inn), refers to a 'drawbridge adjoining to the said gate on the west side on which a shop is now built'.[5] The presence of a drawbridge is now disputed. The arches in the cellar of Chandler's Cottage are simply the remains of the stone bridge which had replaced the original wooden structure. In front of the west tower a substantial house was built, with land running west into the town ditch, which was to be replaced in the early nineteenth century with a set of Gothick legal chambers.

Back in the thirteenth century, the need for walls and gates had become more pressing as the Welsh became increasingly belligerent. Shrewsbury and Hereford had a direct subsidy from the crown to build their walls,[6] but from 1220 most towns raised money themselves by royal assent to 'murage' grants, the right to tax goods brought into the town for sale.[7] With this revenue they paid for their defences. An application was made in 1233 by the people of Ludlow to raise money to build or strengthen their walls. It is not known when work started, but it must have been carried out, for a later application of 1260 was for repairs. By 1283 Edward I had subdued the Welsh, and Wales fell under English rule, but the townspeople of Ludlow still felt insecure, and appealed directly to the king:

> *The people request that they are granted murage for the term of five years so that they are able to rebuild the walls as the people of the country around come to town to save their bodies and their goods and chattels when the Welsh levy war, but the walls are in decay so that people cannot shelter there.*[8]

So, although there was a wall and gates by the time of the murder in 1272, it is not possible to say exactly when the walls had been finished. It is almost certain that around this time there were continuous walls around the town,[9] but, even so, they already required constant maintenance and repair – as they have done ever since.

Ludlow soon took charge of its own affairs. It was a seigneurial borough, but many of its lords were absentees, and the borough came to elect its own community of burgesses who organised the town and became Ludlow Corporation, with twelve Aldermen and twenty-five Common Councillors, headed by High and Low Bailiffs. The town continued into the fifteenth century to pay tolls and burgage rentals to its lords, by this time the Mortimers, until 1462, when Edward IV granted Ludlow its charter. This included the right to take tolls and customs for the repair and fortification of bridges, gates, towers and walls.

As in many walled towns, the fortifications in Ludlow were fronted by a 'fosse' or ditch, crossed at first by wooden bridges at the gates, which were often defended by D-shaped towers. The ditch would have been about twenty-five feet wide, wider in some places. The wall itself was over three feet thick; at the Broad Gate today, it is over twenty feet high from the ditch to the upper level. It would have taken several years to dig the ditch and build the walls round the whole town. Along the ditch to the south-east of the Broad Gate, the wall was built on bedrock which can still be seen. This phase of the work could have been done by local labour, but the building of the towers at the gates was a specialist task, and master masons would have come from elsewhere to construct these where gaps in the walls had been left for them. The D-shaped towers at the Broad Gate are very similar to those at Conway Castle and at Brampton Bryan, and the same itinerant masons may have worked on them all.[10] The towers would have had flat roofs and been joined by a wooden gate below, and at the Broad Gate by a pointed red sandstone arch, with a walkway above which continued along the top of the walls. A tunnel-vaulted passage inside the present house preserves the line of this walkway, linking directly with the line of the garden wall. Originally, the backs of the towers were open, with a staircase cut into the wall, leading from the basement to the top of the east tower. One flight still exists, running down from the kitchen to the cellar. When the towers were filled in with rooms, they may have been roofed and thatched, as they

3. *THE REMAINING MEDIEVAL STEPS*
A flight now leading from the kitchen to the eastern cellar

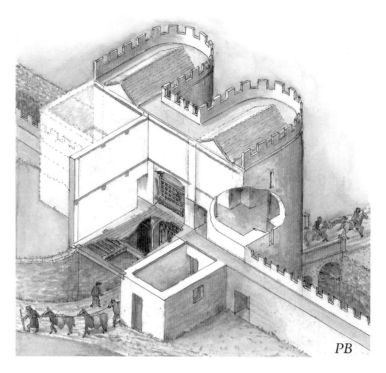

4. *A CUTAWAY OF THE GATEHOUSE*
showing the portcullis, by Peter Brears

were at Galdeford.[11] Between 1270, when there was just a gate across the road, and 1300, the two towers were raised in height, and more buildings appeared on the town side. A portcullis was also added.

The space for this required two more stone arches each side of the original, to trap the portcullis into the grooves which can be seen today. The two outer brick arches appeared in the 1550s, when the building was converted to fill in more of the space between the towers, to extend what is now the kitchen on the south side and support new rooms to the north.

In most walled towns, the walls and gates were soon becoming necessary less for defence and more for show, though they were still useful in guarding against civil unrest. They allowed for the regulation of passage in and out of the town, and above all, for the collection of tolls. New uses were found for the rooms in the towers; they often became chapels, schools or prisons.[12]

In Ludlow, both Corve Gate and Old Gate are said to have had houses built on them in the sixteenth century,[13] though it is not certain that they were substantial dwellings. At the Broad Gate, for many centuries, the rest of the building was leased out for different purposes, but very often on repairing leases. This meant that the Corporation was spared the cost of maintaining the building while at the same time enjoying the rent. The Corporation retained an interest in the basement rooms on either side, often reserving them in leases or including the room at the base of the east tower in the lease of Chandler's Cottage, which had access to it. This area was, for many years, used as a gaol, though there was a larger and more central gaol in the tower at Galdeford Gate, as well as a gaol at the Castle itself, used by the Council in the Marches. In 1554, John Roberts was sentenced to one day in the stocks and four days in Galdeford Tower, but in the same year, one 'Massey' was chained up at the Broad Gate, although he managed to escape by burning down the door.[14] There were many orders in the Corporation Minutes for cleaning the Broad Gate prison and, not surprisingly, for mending its locks. In 1575 the stocks were removed from Old Street to the Broad Gate. The last reference to the gaol comes after the Civil War, when in 1655 an order was given that the Broad Gate was to be used as a House of Correction and repaired for that purpose.[15]

As time went on, changes were made in the west tower. The basement room, at ground level, could be accessed from the central archway as well as from Broad Street; then, at some time, the 'sally-port' was built, which allowed pedestrians and riders on horseback to pass through when the gate was closed. The basement room had its own fireplace. In 1314 Richard de Ashford, a local baker, took a lease on this area of the building, probably for his business. Being built of stone, it was more suitable for his ovens than other wooden buildings in the town.[16] He may also have collected tolls at the gate. In 1482 John Whyte, a tailor, paid the Corporation £4.20s for the right to collect tolls there,[17] and, despite the inflation during the intervening

5. THE THIRTEENTH-CENTURY TOWERS
with buildings added over the years, a drawing dated 1930, by J. Barrie Robinson

period, William Houke did the same in 1572. By this time, the collection of murage and other tolls was regularly farmed out to locals, who paid a fine or tax to the Corporation for the right. These tolls were collected at the main gates.[18] The use of the west tower basement for the collection of tolls continued well into the eighteenth century.

2. THE CONVERSION INTO A HOUSE

In 1301 Edward I had invested his young son Edward, later Edward II, as Prince of Wales. In the fifteenth century this title was given by Edward IV to his own eldest son, Edward, later the short-lived Edward V. Edward IV set up the Council in the Marches in 1471, at first to oversee the estates of the vanquished Mortimers, but then to administer the law over Wales and the Marches and to manage the estates and powers in the area which he had granted to his son, together with the right to keep his court at Ludlow. Ludlow Castle then became the residence for the Prince of Wales. Henry VII and James I would also create their sons, Arthur, Henry and Charles, Princes of Wales, and Henry VIII's daughter, Princess Mary, spent part of her youth at the Castle. So Ludlow had strong royal connections. The role of the Council grew and its powers were increased in 1536, when a new Act of Union led to its statutory recognition. A second Act of Union in 1543 confirmed that the common-law administration of Wales had been transferred to the Council. Though declining in importance, the Council continued until 1641, when it was abolished by the Long Parliament. It was revived with reduced powers under Charles II, but finally closed down in 1689, with the arrival of William and Mary.

The presence of the Council had attracted considerable numbers of lawyers and administrators to Ludlow. They built large houses and brought a more sophisticated world to provincial Shropshire. In the sixteenth century important families like the Sidneys and the Townshends gave status to the town. Sir Henry Sidney was Lord President of the Council from 1559-86, and the tomb of his daughter, Ambrosia, is in the chancel of St Laurence's. He oversaw 'the great rebuilding' at the Castle, though he spent most of his time in London. At first, the grand houses of other officials were located at the centre of the town, near the Castle, the church and the market place. Charles Fox, Secretary of the Council in the 1550s, built his 'fayre' house with its courtyard in Quality Square; Rees Jones, a lawyer for the Council, on his marriage, converted and embellished a house in the Bull Ring, which is now the Feathers Hotel. But in the later sixteenth century, Broad Street was becoming a fashionable part of the town.

Around 1570, Edmund Walter, a member of the Council and Chief Justice for South Wales, built a new brick house at the south-west end of Broad Street, on a site now occupied by numbers 35, 36 and 37. Brick was a new material in Ludlow, but had been used from the mid-sixteenth century onwards, for instance in Charles Fox's house in Quality Square. The new building was described by Thomas Churchyard in his poem 'The Worthiness of Wales' (1587) as 'the fayre house by the gate by the making of Mr Justice Walter'.[19] His house would have looked directly at the Broad Gate, which by this time was two hundred and fifty years old and in poor repair. In February 1565, Edmund Walter took out a lease which included the whole building apart from the rooms at the base of the towers. It was a repairing lease, and he agreed to pull down 'all the timber work of the gate' and to rebuild the 'overhouse'.[20] Presumably, he wanted to improve the view from his windows. It was probably at this stage that the area between the towers was further filled in and new rooms built on the north side. An indenture of 1572 granting William Houke a parcel of ground west of the Broad Gate, refers to 'the new building over the said Brodgate'.[21]

Nowadays, there are three gables on the south-facing roof. These were fashionable additions to a house at the time, and they probably appeared when Edmund Walter's new rooms were built, at the same time as the new brick arches. There would have been similar gables on the north side of the roof which no longer exist. They were either destroyed in the fire of 1700, or removed as part of the mid-eighteenth-century alterations.

By the late sixteenth century, the Broad Gate had became a much more useful set of premises, though it may not yet have been a house to live in. In 1592, John Harrison was renting 'a tenement over the gate'. He is described as 'Master to the children', so it is likely that he kept a school there.[22] The accommodation was obviously quite substantial: in 1598 Thomas Saunders, gentleman, paid the Corporation 12s. per annum 'for all that house, edifice and building erected or being over a gate commonly called or known as Bradgate...with all and every room and chamber to keep in repair'.[23] Samuel Lloyd, gentleman, took a lease on the building in the early 1600s;[24] and Richard Dalton, a cleric who became Rector of Stoke Edith in 1596, and in 1614 a canon of Hereford Cathedral, in 1601 leased a tenement in Broad Street 'with a building and rooms over the Broad Gate'. He renewed the lease together with one on the house next door, No. 33, in 1615.[25] Four years later, his widow renewed the lease, but she may have resided at No. 33. Around 1610, John Ludnam took over Samuel Lloyd's lease, renewing it in 1631,[26] but since, after 1614, Richard Dalton also had a lease, they must have used different parts of the building. It is not certain that anyone actually lived in the Broad Gate itself during these years, but in 1634, the Corporation was supplying 'twelve pounds of good tallow candles' to light the gate in the winter, between the feast of All Saints and the purification of the Blessed Virgin Mary, every morning and every evening, according to the will of Charles Nixon.[27]

John Ludnam was a musician. He was one of the Shrewsbury Town Waits,[28] watchmen who also played instruments, and he may have performed in Ludlow as well. The waits wore livery and silver chains bearing the town's coat of arms and played at important public occasions. John Ludnam appears to have been the chief wait, as he paid for some of their livery himself, and the waits are often referred to as 'Ludnam's men'.[29] On 4th November, 1616, Charles, son of James I, was invested as Prince of Wales at Whitehall. On the same day there were celebrations in Ludlow. They started with the affixing of the arms, name and style of the prince under the pulpit in St Laurence's church, in the Castle chapel, in the court-house, and on the town gates. About nine o'clock in the morning, a procession of richly-apparelled town officials entered the Castle. Before them went the town waits; and a procession headed by two hundred soldiers. On the Castle green they met similarly-dressed officials of the Council in the Marches, and 'another company [of] waits and good consorts of Musicke with various wind instruments'. These parties processed to the church with 'instruments playing and sounding all along the way before them'.[30] John Ludnam almost certainly took part in these events.

During the Civil War, Ludlow was a Royalist stronghold, inhabited at times by Prince Rupert and visited by the King. The townspeople inside the walls were protected, but under constant threat, and those outside were ordered to dig their own fortifications. By 1646 Shrewsbury and Bridgnorth had fallen to the Parliamentarians, and Ludlow was under siege. Corve Gate was described in 1647 as 'ruined in these unnatural wars',[31] but, as it turned out, the Broad Gate was not stormed by the enemy. Negotiations took place and Ludlow surrendered on 1st June 1646. There was considerable damage to the houses below the Broad Gate in the town ditch, either from the Parliamentarians, or because some were deliberately burned down by the Royalists to give them a better line of fire, but the Gate itself seems to have survived unscathed.

In May 1647 a certain William Beddoe or Beddoes complained that he had been imprisoned 'for a roundhead in the martiall's [sic] ward of Ludlow when the King's army was in these parts'.[32] He said that he had been forced to relinquish his tenements and flee malicious persecution, but had returned after the 'reducement' of the town. His father, Ellis Beddoe, had been High Bailiff in 1624 and 1635, and had apparently owned or leased various properties in Ludlow which passed to his son. 'Widow Ludnam' at one time had a lease on a 'house above the Broadgate'; which 'Wm Bedoe doth live in and sayth he hath bought Ludnam's life'. Richard Collier was the leaseholder at the Broad Gate from 1672 onwards, and in his renewal of the lease in 1684 for 'rooms over the Broad Gate', the previous leaseholder is said to have been 'formerly William Beddoes'. Richard Collier was another leaseholder who had a repairing lease. In 1672 he was required to 'get possession' of the building and put it 'in sufficient repair within two years', but it is not known what he used it for.[33] In May 1673, John Chandler also took a lease of rooms over the Broad Gate.[34] Apart, perhaps, from William Beddoe, it is not certain that any of these leaseholders actually used the Broad Gate as their main residence.

From 1688 to 1693 the next leaseholder was William Palmer, who was sexton at St.Laurence's Church, and who had trained as a gunsmith. He also worked on the Church's clock and chimes and provided a turret clock for the Grammar School at the bottom of Mill Street. In April 1688 the Corporation granted him a lease for the Broad Gate at the previous rent of twelve shillings a year, on condition that he took on the task of 'putting the said house in repayre'.[35] He does not seem to have lived at the Broad Gate. He had a house in the Bull Ring, and the Poll Tax register for 1689 confirms that there was still no one resident at the Broad Gate. It is possible that, although the word in the Corporation Minute Book is 'repayre', the work that William carried out was more fundamental. His series of 'repayres' was completed by January 1693, when he paid a sixpenny fine, i.e. tax, and was given permission to pass on the lease of the Broad Gate to John Stead,[36] who appears to have been the first person to regard the whole property as a potential dwelling house for himself and his family.

6. *A BLIND WINDOW ON THE FRONT OF THE HOUSE*
This no longer functions, and is all that remains on the exterior
of the early eighteenth-century house built by John Stead

− 1 −

THE STEADS
1693-1725

When the Council of the Marches was abolished in 1689, many lawyers and other officials moved back to London, leaving their large houses behind. This allowed wealthy families in the surrounding area to lease or buy them to use as 'town houses'. After the Great Fire of 1666, houses in London had to be built or rebuilt of brick or stone rather than wood, and a classical style of architecture prevailed. In Ludlow, this change of taste and the desire to be up-to-date with London fashions, meant that brick, stone and sash windows were widely adopted.

Several families simply re-fronted their houses. At the start of the eighteenth century two adjacent timber-framed houses in Broad Street were knocked down and a fine stone house, 27 Broad Street, was built in their place. At about the same time, 40 Broad Street was improved and re-fronted using brick. The change from one style to the other meant that at times Broad Street must have looked like a building site. As late as 19th May 1756, when 35, 36 and 37 were being built immediately outside the Broad Gate, on the site of Edmund Walter's house, the Corporation ordered that 'Mr Dunne be wrote to that unless he directly remove the rubbish he hath laid in the street and make satisfaction for the damage done thereby to the street, he will be sued'.[37]

This kind of building activity in the town from the end of the seventeenth century may have influenced the transformation of the Broad Gate into a residence. When its role as part of the town's defences ceased after the Civil War, it was subsequently used as a base for whoever contracted to collect the tolls and 'murage'. The leasing of the gates for 'portership', that is the right to open, close and control entry through the gate, was on the wane, however, as the Tolsey in the Bull Ring was taking over the collection of tolls, which finally ceased in 1827. The prison at the base of the east tower had long become redundant. These developments caused the Broad Gate to be seen as a possible gentleman's town house, located as it was on an important site at one end of the town's most prestigious street. Around 1688 its new status was reflected in the leases for the Broad Gate that had once referred to 'rooms above the gate' and now described the building as a 'house' or 'dwelling house'.

In legal documents John Stead was often referred to as 'Doctor Stead', which suggests that he was a trained physician. In the 1693 lease he is referred to as 'John Stead, apothecary', but he had been licensed as a physician five years earlier in 1688 to practise medicine in the dioceses of Hereford, St. David's and Worcester. At the time, all medical practitioners had to be licensed by the archbishop or his representative. Testimonial letters had to be provided, certifying their ability and their adherence to the Church of England. They were then required to take the oaths of Allegiance and Supremacy. Letters on behalf of John Stead were signed by Hugh Chamberlain and Gideon Harvey, both very distinguished medical men of their day.[38] Along with his medical practice, however, he was something of a property developer.

With the main house at the Broad Gate, Dr Stead also took on 'the dungeon, the messe place before the door on the east side, together with the two cottages and gardens of the widows Walker and Benson'. A later lease confirms that these cottages were in Maryvale (the area on the town side of the wall between Broad Street and Mill Street, once called Barnaby Lane, and nowadays Silk Mill Lane). As was usual, the lease was for thirty-one years and the annual rent was now seventeen shillings.[39]

The Stead family probably had their roots in Yorkshire, in Ilkley or Otley. They moved to North Herefordshire and South Shropshire in the early seventeenth century, but appear to have kept their Yorkshire connection. Anthony Stead, whose son was born in Ludlow in 1642, died in Yorkshire in 1644, and Thomas Stead of Pembridge took his son John to be baptised there in 1715. Anthony Stead might have been related to the Walter Stead who was one of the town Bailiffs in 1648. Along with several other men, Walter was charged with 'delinquency' after the Civil War, but was later restored to favour. He had married Margery Vaughan in 1625, and was the uncle of John Stead, a confectioner in London, to whom he had left money in his will. This London-based John Stead was the father of Dr John Stead who acquired the lease of the Broad Gate in 1693.

The Ludlow parish records for 1681 show that Dr Stead was appointed a churchwarden for St Laurence's. At the time, this post was recognised as the start of the route to membership of a position within Ludlow Corporation, but although Dr Stead was duly elected to the Corporation in the following year, he held no office and in 1696 'forfeited his place by not subscribing to the Association according to [the] late Act of Parliament'.[40] This act had been passed in the April of that year. These were difficult and uncertain years, when plots against the new protestant king, William III, were instigated by the exiled James II, with the support of the French king, Louis XIV. 'For the better security of his Majesty's person', all office-holders were required to make a declaration or be fined for suggesting that William was not the rightful monarch. This was clearly a step too far for Dr Stead, who had sworn allegiance to James II. His refusal to make this declaration may have halted his progress in the Corporation, but it did not stop him from continuing to acquire land and properties in Ludlow. He was able to do so more easily because some of the land was already mortgaged to his father, the London confectioner.

In the late seventeenth century there were few if any banks in the provinces where families could deposit money, so it was common for those with spare funds to invest in property, and property conferred status. Dr Stead had been doing this since 1684, when he leased and rebuilt 2-3 Brand Lane. He followed this by applying to build a summer-house in the garden.[41] In 1685 he bought the extensive former Austin Priory site in Lower Galdeford, together with six other properties which had once been owned by the friars. Some were burgage plots in Old Street; others were fields, including the 'Great Meadow'. This large area, about eleven acres, almost one twentieth of the borough, had once been owned by the Townshend family; it then passed through Henry Barnard to Humphrey Bradshaw before Dr Stead purchased it. It may have included the remains of the large house built by Robert Townshend fifty years earlier from the ruins of the Austin Priory, and said to have been burnt down after the Civil War.[42] By 1694, John Stead had added Sutton's Close, just under two acres of adjoining land, which he bought from William Archer, former Clerk at the Council in the Marches.[43] The Poll Tax register of 1689 shows him living at the west end of Drapers' Row (now King Street) with his wife, Priscilla, née Pulley, his two surviving children, Edward and John, an apprentice and a maid.

When in 1693 John Stead acquired the lease of the Broad Gate from the gunsmith, William Palmer, he paid the same rent, 17s. p.a., but he also acquired the leases of the town ditch and the land on the wall to the west of the house, so that it became one property, for which he paid 32s. The Broad Gate now had a garden. At first, like William Palmer, he did not live in the house. According to the 1692 Poll Tax Register, he was still at his old address in Drapers' Row, this time with his wife and one child. Between 1686 and 1690 John Stead and his wife lost five children, Elizabeth, George, Alathea, Valentine and Isaac. In February 1691 their eldest son, Edward, died, and in

1692 their youngest daughter, Alice. They were left with only their second son, John, who was followed later by four other children, a second Elizabeth, Anne, a second Edward and a second Valentine, all of whom reached adulthood and spent their childhood at the Broad Gate.

In addition to practising medicine and busily acquiring property in Ludlow, John Stead had in 1686 also taken on the job of keeping the 'streets and lands within the walls' clear of 'all heaps of dirt', and in 1690 he was allowed to create a sewer under Broad Street and Brand Lane. The entry in the Corporation Minutes for 29th May 1690 reads:

> *Order that leave be given to Mr John Stead to make a common shore [sewer] in the Broad Street and leading throw [through] and under the Brand Lane, he keeping the grate of the shore from being noysome or offensive.*[44]

Dr Stead was a litigious character and was involved in several Chancery Court cases, one of which concerned the Broad Gate. Instead of moving at once into the house, when he acquired the lease in 1693, he carried on the work of converting it into a family residence. He and his family may have been there by 1699, when he paid a land tax of 13s. However, a major fire at the house around 1700 meant that he had to rebuild the premises. He was clearly from a wealthy family, and it is reasonable to assume that he usually contracted a number of craftsmen for the work on his houses. Certainly in 1696 he had employed William Piper and his band of workmen. William was a plasterer, but working for him were men of various trades, who between them carried out a great deal of work for John Stead. In 1708 Piper brought a lawsuit, claiming that the cost of the work done by his men totalled £14.3s 3d., but that he had received only £8.17s. The case went to the Court of Chancery in London. John Stead's defence was that, 'Twelve years ago I employed William Piper of Ludlow, plasterer, to sile [seal] walls and plaster with lime and mortar certain rooms chambers and other buildings in my then dwelling house in Ludlow which he did and I paid him what his work was worth but taking advantage of the fact that I paid him without witnesses he claims I did not. He overcharged me. Now he sues me in the town court'. In his deposition Piper detailed some of the work that he carried out, although it is not absolutely clear that this was all work on the Broad Gate and, because of the fire and later alterations, it is not possible to identify most of the details. The particulars of the rooms worked on were given as follows:

The Study: *plastered walls to top siled and hung and presse for books; plastered corishes [cornices]*

Hall: *Ovals of fretwork 4 in each corner and one large one in middle a cove cornice in plaster on top of wall in imitation of wainscot and panelling 18 or 19 feet long*

Gallery: *turned in 3 curtle arches in plaster mantels and each side sealed underneath*

Chamber: *next to the Study: ceiling and cornice with 2 coats walls with one hung with two beds*

Closet: *adjoining it: plastered and ceiled*

Parlour: *ceiled and chimney set in Dutch Style [fireplace with Delft tiles]*

Kitchen: *walls plastered ceiling whitened*

Next Room: *the like*

Room over kitchen: *walls plastered*

2 Cellars and Buttery: *ceiled*

Servants [workmen] and Wages:
    John Hill 8d per day; William Piper [his son?] 8d per day; James Perks 10d per day; George Farr 10d per day; myself 10d.

More work at the plaintiff's Summer House in the Burnt [Brand] Lane 1s 6d.[45]

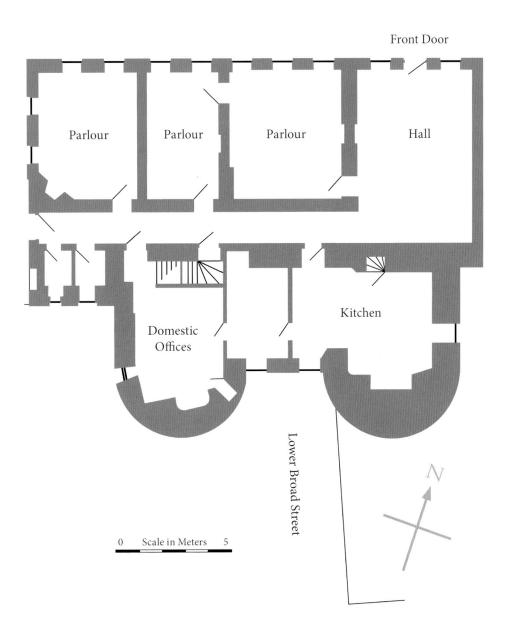

Front Door

Parlour

Parlour

Parlour

Hall

Domestic
Offices

Kitchen

Lower Broad Street

N

0   Scale in Meters   5

A GROUND FLOOR PLAN OF THE STEAD HOUSE
as rebuilt after the fire of 1700

If this had been a twenty-first-century bill, the labour charges would have been higher than the cost of materials, but if it is assumed that only half of this bill of over £14 was for wages and the other half went on the wood, plaster and other materials, then John Stead had contracted for about one hundred and seventy man-days of work. This would have meant five or six weeks' full-time work for the five workmen including William. In that time they would have completed a good deal of rebuilding and improvement.

In his deposition to the Court of Chancery John Stead referred to the fire of 1700. William Piper at the same court confirmed that there had been a fire in the premises, when 'a great part of the house burnt down but was not totally consumed, part of the walls remaining and later being repaired'. It must have been repaired quickly, as the Stead family, now with their four younger children, moved in, and, in 1705, John Stead paid window tax for thirty-five panes. Nearly three hundred years later, in 1992, when work was being carried out in the house, signs of a fire were discovered in the cellar at the north-east end. A substantial beam which had been blackened and charred by flames was crumbling and had to be replaced.

It is obvious today that the eastern end of the building above the cellar is more recent than the main body of the house; the style and size of the windows suggest that it is part of the mid-eighteenth-century renovation. Further to the west, though, one feature which certainly remains from John Stead's time is the middle window with two twelve-pane sashes on the first floor of the north front. Judging from the windows on the first floor at 35 and 36 Broad Street, which we know to have been built in 1756, the windows each side with thick glazing bars would seem to belong to the early to mid-eighteenth century, while the windows to the hall and drawing room below must have been changed again at a later date.

The extensive panoramic view of Ludlow from Whitcliffe, painted for the Salweys of Richard's Castle in 1722 by Isaac Vogelsanck and Bernard Lens, shows the garden front of the house that John Stead built, with the gable end

7. *A DETAIL FROM THE VOGELSANCK PANORAMA*
showing the garden side of the house in 1722, before additions to the north and south

of the west elevation and the western drum tower, much as it appears today, without the additional brick building to the north or the Gothick extension to the south. There appear to be windows looking west from a bedroom, but, judging from the window surround found in a cupboard in that room, there must have been more on the north front than there are now. So the

41

windows probably ran along the whole of the north front, which stretched, unbroken, from one side of the arch to the other and may have extended equally and symmetrically on both sides. The front door then could only have been placed at the east arm of the house, facing north, where the raised bank above the road leads to the pavement up Broad Street.

The Eye branch of the Stead family became an important local firm of builders, particularly in the nineteenth century. Samuel Stead, master stonemason, was highly regarded by C. R. Cockerell (1788-1863), a leading architect of his day. He built his own house at 16 Castle Square in 1838. His brother, Matthew, of Stead and Son Builders, designed the Ludlow Assembly Rooms in 1837 and the Workhouse in about 1839; his son, also Matthew, went to Canada, where he became a highly successful architect. Another Stead, James, born in Ashford, is described as a builder in Tenbury Wells in the 1881 Census. There must be many houses in Ludlow and the surrounding area built by the Stead family. But the Steads were not all developers and builders. We have seen that Dr Stead's father was a London confectioner, though he kept an interest in land in Ludlow. Dr Stead himself was, of course, a medical man. One of his younger sons, Edward, was a clockmaker. He was apprenticed in 1716 to Thomas Vernon, clock and watchmaker, who was twice High Bailiff of Ludlow, for a premium of £20.[46] The eldest surviving son, John, appears to have followed his father into the medical profession.

A legal document of 1729 concerning the sale of land refers to 'John Stead the younger, late of the city of London, doctor of Physick'.[47] There is no record, however, that he was medically qualified. He had, however, been a Fellow of All Souls College, Oxford, 'the son of John Stead of Ludlow, Gent.' He had matriculated at Balliol College, Oxford, in 1701, probably from Ludlow Grammar School, which had a close connection with the college. He took his BA degree in 1705 and, after several attempts, was elected to All Souls on November 4th 1709. He became an MA in the same year. In 1717 he was a Proctor of the university, and so a Delegate of the University Press, and was also elected bursar of his college, his original seven-year fellowship having run out.[48]

It is still possible, though, that he was intending to become a doctor. As a young fellow of an Oxford college, he would have been expected to remain celibate and take Holy Orders. If he wished to marry, he would have had to to leave the college and move to a living. Clearly, John Stead did not wish to follow this route. In 1714, he applied for a dispensation from Holy Orders, which was possible for those intending to be doctors or lawyers. By doing so he aroused the hostility of Warden Gardiner, who was bitterly opposed to fellows being dispensed from what he saw as an essential requirement for fulfilling the wishes of the founder for a college of priests, a pious community of scholars. There were already four medical fellows (a large number for an Oxford college at the time), and he saw no reason to add to their number. He found ammunition in a complaint from the Rev. William Piers and his brother, John Piers. They were the grandsons of William Piers, Bishop of Peterborough, who had been Vice-Chancellor of Oxford from 1621-24. Their complaint was that John Piers's two daughters, Barbara and Mary, were kept at John Stead's house in Pirton, ten miles from Oxford, and that he 'cohabits with … Mrs [mistress] Barbara Piers – but denies marriage to her'.[49] Gardiner's case was that if Stead was married, he could not continue as a fellow, and if he was not, then he was guilty of immorality. John Stead's defence was that he had moved away from Oxford for the sake of his health, and that he had at first lodged with Barbara's family at Denton, where he had been seen walking with her 'in the filbert grove', but had become guardian and protector to the two sisters when it was clear that their uncle, father and stepmother neglected and exploited them and wished to appropriate their estate. This had been left to them by their aunt, Alice Darryl, who had brought them up, and her dying wish was that they should not live with their father while their stepmother was alive. In 1715 John Stead was prosecuted by Barbara Piers's father and uncle in the university's Chancellor's Court, but he declared that he had appealed to the Visitor of the College, who had found in his favour, and the case was dismissed for 'want of prosecution'.

When he was elected Bursar by a majority of the fellows, but without the Warden's vote, Dr Gardiner, with whom he was now on very bad terms, charged him with embezzlement.[50] In March 1717 the new Visitor, Archbishop Wake, upheld his appointment as bursar, but reprimanded him for his behaviour to the Warden. He seems to have been popular with the young fellows, however, who described him in a letter written on his behalf to the Visitor as 'one of the soberest, most studious, modest and most virtuous young men'. The antiquarian, Thomas Hearne, remembered him as 'a worthy good sort of man'.[51] He continued to reject the Warden's authority by taking leave of absence without permission, and spending time in London 'attending his patients', but was advised by the Vicar General, Dr Bettesworth, to return. He said that he had already booked his place 'on the flying coach' and would 'give your Grace no further trouble'. In any case, he was replaced as bursar in 1718, and no more is heard of him at All Souls.[52] He went ahead with his marriage to Barbara Piers and, with her sister, they moved to London, where he continued his medical career. He died of a fever there in October 1718. In his will he left his estate to his wife, 'Barbara Stead (late Barbara Piers)', and his 'books and instruments' to his brother, Valentine.

The absence of any record for the younger John Stead's qualifying as a doctor is understandable, since he died so young. It was perfectly acceptable at the time for episcopal licences to be applied for after some years of practice, and such licences were seen more as 'certificates of honesty and good conduct'.[53] An indication that John had trained as a doctor is his request in his will that his wife and her sister should be allowed to live, until either of them should remarry, with 'Dr Bright', to whom he had probably been apprenticed. More conclusive evidence is provided by his entry in the parish register for St Paul's, Covent Garden, where he was buried on 10th October,

1718, which describes him as 'John Stead, Doctor of Physic'. In the legal document of 1729 his brother Edward is described as his heir; presumably he inherited after Barbara's death.

Although he sold much of his land to Edward Waring in 1729, including the house, 'Friars', in Sutton's Close, Dr John Stead the elder had, by 1720, acquired the lease of 32 Broad Street, but continued to pay window tax for the Broad Gate and to live there. His first lease expired in 1723, and on 23rd October 1724, now described as 'Doctor of Physick', he took a new lease on the property. This consisted of a 'messuage [dwelling-house] over and adjoining Broadgate, court before same, stable/garden/backside (on which a dwelling formerly stood), messplace [forecourt] and garden in Merrivale, backside and garden in the town ditch (formerly Edward Harris, tailor)'. He was to pay an annual rent of 32s. At the same time the interest on a fine of £5 was remitted, because he had rebuilt the house after the fire. The Corporation held on to the dungeon at the base of the east tower, which was now no longer part of the Broad Gate lease, but included in the lease for Chandler's Cottage, later part of the Wheatsheaf Inn.[54]

The dungeon was still 'reserved' in a later lease of the inn issued by the Corporation in 1806. In John Stead's time and after, the room in the west tower for the collector of tolls also continued to be in use. In 1717 Edward Harris, the tailor, who lived nearby, was granted 'the tolls of Broadstreet gate' for three years, paying £10 a year quarterly. A new lease was then granted to him every three years until it was renewed for nine years in 1732.[55] The last surviving grant of the right to collect tolls at the Broad Gate was in 1741, when John Colerick took on a nine year lease.[56] He was a blacksmith and lived in a house 'adjoining' the Broad Gate, probably the house built against the south front of the west tower.

In the Easter Book for 1724, Dr Stead, physician, is described as living in the house with his wife, daughter and a maid. His elder daughter Elizabeth had already married Thomas Wellings, so this daughter would have been

Anne. His sons, in their twenties, had previously left home. In his will, drawn up in 1738, he left all his goods to his unmarried daughter, Anne, with 1s each to his remaining three children, Edward, Valentine and Elizabeth. John himself lived on until 1741, but after the death of his wife, Priscilla, in 1724, he lived elsewhere, perhaps 32 Broad Street. In 1725 he petitioned the Corporation to 'alien' his lease; and by the following year the Broad Gate was in the hands of the Sprotts.[57]

— 2 —

THE SPROTTS
1726-1784

In 1726 the tax on thirty-one windows at the Broad Gate was paid by 'Madam Sprott'. 'Madam' or 'Dame' was a courtesy title given at the time to gentry widows and female relatives of a certain age. In 1729 she was just 'Mrs Sprott', and in 1731 she was described as 'Joyce Sprott, widow'. The Sprotts were a minor gentry family who lived at the Marsh, in Barrow, near Much Wenlock. In the mid-seventeenth century Henry Sprott, who came from Ashmore Brook near Lichfield in Staffordshire, had acquired the Marsh through his wife Anne, daughter of Thomas Lockier. The Sprotts owned considerable amounts of land in Staffordshire and surrounding counties, and Henry's father, Edward, had died fighting on the royalist side at the battle of Marston Moor, but the Lockiers were of older gentry stock and had built a large house at Barrow. Nowadays the Marsh is a late-eighteenth-century red brick farmhouse, but parts of the Lockier mansion are still visible in a sixteenth-century stone range on the west side of the forecourt.[58] In 1672 it was taxed on thirteen hearths.

Henry Sprott married Anne Lockier at Barrow church in September 1654. They had at least four daughters, and a surviving son, Thomas, born in 1667, who matriculated at Oxford in 1683 and became a student at the Inner Temple in 1686. On 19th February 1690, at Barrow, Thomas married Joyce

8. THE MARSH, NEAR BARROW
The Shropshire home of the Sprotts from 1654 to 1801. Now an eighteenth-century farmhouse,
but remains of the Lockier mansion can be seen on the right

Bowdler, daughter of Samuel Bowdler of Barrow and Ludlow. They had two sons and five daughters. The Bowdlers were a well-established Ludlow family of mercers, and the Sprotts had close connections with Ludlow. Thomas and Joyce's eldest son, another Henry, had been elected an honorary burgess of Ludlow Corporation in 1722,[59] and members of the Sprott family were already living in the town, spread out between Mill Street and Broad Street. Anne Sprott, née Lockier, Thomas's widowed mother, is recorded in the 1692 Poll Tax returns as living at 8 Mill Street, where she stayed until her death in 1721. The Mill Street house seems to have been a kind of dower house for the Sprott widows. When Anne's daughter-in-law, Joyce, was widowed, she lived there with her daughters and her son, Samuel, until they moved into the Broad Gate in 1726. In 1724 her sisters-in-law, Isabella, Mary and Anne, were living at 17 Broad Street. After Mary and Anne married, Isabella lived

48

there alone as a spinster until she was joined by her widowed nephew, John Baldwin. She also had a mortgage on 9 Castle Street from 1727 to 1733. In the 1760s, one of Thomas and Joyce's daughters, another Isabella, moved to 23 Broad Street, a freehold owned by the Sprotts, which she shared with her sister, Elizabeth. Thomas's grand-daughter, another Elizabeth, married a wealthy solicitor from London, William Toldervy, and lived first at 36 and then 38 Broad Street, which her husband rebuilt. Their nephew, George, later lived at 18 Broad Street. Dorothy Ashwood, another grand-daughter, in 1765 was paying window tax on 39 Broad Street, which she bought for £500, with the help of the lawyer, Somerset Davies, who lived at number 27. After her death, her executors sold it in 1784 to Admiral James Vashon for £599. The Sprott family also held the lease of the Wheatsheaf Inn. William Toldervy's lease on Chandler's Cottage was renewed in 1748; and by 1800 Elizabeth Toldervy was also the owner of the Angel Inn.[60]

All the Sprotts seem to have invested heavily in property and their acquisitions passed frequently between family members. Mary Sprott, Samuel Sprott's widow, owned or leased 9 Broad Street from 1767 to 1770. Elizabeth Toldervy, her niece by marriage, also a widow, owned it from 1784 to 1797, and Elizabeth's brother-in-law, James Moseley, from 1797 to 1801. Another acquisition, 78-82 Holdgate Fee, south of the town wall, was owned by Samuel Sprott from 1756 to 1760. Margery Moseley, his niece Anne's mother-in-law, owned it from 1760 to 1782 and William Toldervy, his niece Elizabeth's husband, from 1782 to 1806. The Sprotts, of course, also had large estates in Shropshire and Staffordshire, and, as in many families, land was a cause of contention. In 1746 a case was heard in the Court of Chancery in London between Samuel Sprott, Bachelor in Physick, and James Moseley and his wife, Anne.[61] She was one of the three daughters of Samuel's late brother Henry, and she and her husband were disputing the right and title to property in the manor of Longdon in Staffordshire. It is not clear how the case ended, but in his will, drawn up in 1753, Samuel stipulated that 'in case

Mrs Moseley or her husband shall make any claim or disturbance against the testator's heir, devisee or executrix, he revokes any devise, gift or legacy herein given.' This was not the only Chancery case fought over land by members of the family against each other. In 1798-1800, the Moseleys were taken to court by Thomas Yate, who had inherited Samuel Sprott's estate.[62]

Thomas Sprott had four sisters, five daughters and at least three granddaughters so, together with the widows, there were a great many women in the Sprott family and it is remarkable how often they bought property or took out leases or mortgages independently of their male relatives. Most women suffered financially if they were unmarried or widowed, but in Ludlow, in 1763, sixty-three per cent of heads of households were women, mostly widows.[63] In the absence of male heirs, they could be left land and property, and the Sprott ladies were well provided for by the terms of their fathers' or husbands' wills or marriage settlements. They were able to live comfortably and to spend their own money as they pleased. Dorothy Ashwood, for instance, in a deed of settlement of 1747, was left an annuity of £60 a year, the equivalent of many thousands in today's money. She had inherited most of her mother Anne Sprott's personal estate when she died in 1763, and, through her husband, she had interests in Madeley and Ironbridge. She owned 39 Broad Street, where she lived, and a house with some land in the town ditch to the west of the Broad Gate, which she let. She also at one time shared the lease of the Wheatsheaf Inn with Samuel and Mary Sprott. The younger Joyce Sprott, her cousin, also bought her own house. In their wills they were able to specify legacies which were not to be appropriated by husbands. Earlier, Alice Dawes (John Stead's sister-in-law) had left many of her possessions to her sister, Priscilla Stead, 'to her own proper use and dispose for ever'. Among the Sprott womenfolk. Anne Pryce had left her niece, Mary Hall, 'forty shillings yearly & every year during the term of her life, to be paid to her own Hands & for her own use, & her acquittance shall be sufficient discharge without her Husband'. Her niece, Anne Yate, was to have the interest on the residue of her estate, again 'without her husband'. Later, in 1797, Joyce Sprott the younger left the rents of her dwelling-house to her niece, Mary Ann Wheeler, making it very clear that it was 'for the term of her natural life to and for her own separate use and disposal and wherewith her present and any future husband shall not intermeddle within, shall the same or any part thereof be subject to any of his or their debts, forfeiture, management or control'. The independence of women was greatly valued in the Sprott family and they generally insisted on their rights. Joyce Sprott senior, Thomas's widow of fifteen years, was living with her son Samuel, her daughters and their aunts at 8 Mill Street in 1724, but by 1726 she had moved with Samuel and four of her daughters into the Broad Gate, where the Stead lease still had twenty-nine years to run. When John Stead applied to alienate the lease to the Sprotts in 1725, the name 'Samuel, Dr of Physick' was crossed out and the name of his mother, 'Joyce, widow' firmly substituted.

The strength of character of the Sprott widows is most clearly seen in some of their wills. Without their husbands, they now had absolute freedom to dispose of any unentailed estates in any way they wished, and also to exercise power over their relatives in the future, to reward their favourite nephews and nieces or to pay off old scores. Anne Pryce's generous bequest to her 'beloved nephew, Samuel Sprott', depended on his agreeing to be her executor, 'as he has promised, and as I most earnestly desire'. If he refused, he would get much less. In spite of 'the many and uncommon afflictions' and 'unjust troubles' that she suffered, she lived to be ninety-one, still claiming to be 'of sound sense and perfect and good memory'. The wording of her will reveals her to be an intelligent and articulate woman with a strong religious faith, and very much in control to the end of her life.

Joyce Sprott's elder son, Henry, who had inherited the Marsh, was in Holy Orders, and Samuel, her second son, was a physician. Both brothers married sisters from the Childe family of Kinlet, not far from Barrow. There were

9. THE BIRCH, NEAR KINLET
the home of Thomas Childe and his family, where Mary Sprott grew up

only two years in age between the brothers, but whereas Henry married Anne in Kinlet on 10th June 1718, Samuel's marriage to Mary took place twenty-five years later at Bromfield in February 1743. The father of Anne and Mary, Thomas Childe, who was also in Holy Orders, had inherited the family home of Birch, near Kinlet, and was Sheriff of Shropshire in 1705, but died young in 1708. He was the younger son of Sir William Childe, Master in Chancery, and brother of Sir Lacon Childe who rebuilt Kinlet Hall, a fine Palladian house of about 1727-29, by Francis Smith of Warwick. Anne and Mary's brother, William Lacon Childe, inherited the title and the house from his uncle. Through their mother, Sarah, daughter of Sir Edward Acton of Aldenham, the children were linked to another important Shropshire family. The Sprott brothers had married well and moved up the social scale.

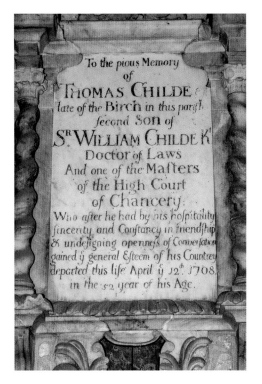

*10. MEMORIAL TO THOMAS CHILDE
in Kinlet church, emphasising his
distinguished father*

It may have been a desire to keep up with his in-laws and to please his new wife that would later lead to Samuel's ambitious alterations to the Broad Gate, including its Gothick frontage, its grand entrance hall and its imposing staircase.

Joyce Sprott had died in 1732. In her will she passed on the lease of the Broad Gate to 'her son, Samuel Sprott, doctor', subject to a legacy of £100 to her unmarried daughter, Elizabeth, with 'the bed and furniture in his room ... and scrutor [escritoire or desk]'. After Samuel married Mary, a marriage settlement was drawn up in 1745.[64] Mary had brought with her a marriage portion of £3,000, which would be equivalent to a large six-figure sum in today's money. Samuel by now was about to inherit the Marsh from his brother Henry, who had recently died. He also owned the family home, Ashmore Brook, with other land in Staffordshire, including the manor of Longdon, together with property in Coalbrookdale. He held the lease of the Broad Gate and in 1747 acquired 'the dwelling-house near the same with orchard and garden belonging' (the cottage attached to the front of the west tower), which was let at the time to Roger Harding. He also held the lease of the Wheatsheaf Inn, Shenstone's Yard in Upper Galdeford, and some meadows around Ludlow. So they were a very prosperous couple and

11. KINLET HALL
built by Sir Lacon Childe in 1727-9, and inherited by William Lacon Childe,
brother of Anne and Mary Sprott

ample provision was made for any children they might have. At the time of their marriage, Samuel was aged forty-seven and his wife forty. After the death of their mother his sisters had married or moved, and he had lived until his marriage alone at the Broad Gate, in the house that John Stead had rebuilt. He now needed to update his residence. In 1731 tax had been paid on thirty-one windows, but by 1748 there were thirty-seven. At some point during these years or after, there was a major renovation of the house.

It is likely that these alterations, both external and internal, were designed by the Shrewsbury architect, Thomas Farnolls Pritchard (1723-1777). They include the battlemented pediment to the north front of the house, matching the battlements on the south-facing drum towers, and crowned with a triangular panel composed of two double Ss back to back, the unusual front door surround, and the addition of an oak staircase and classical arches in the hall. The realignment of the first floor bedrooms, probably the result of having to fit in the new staircase, suggests that there were one or even two more windows on the north front going west, though now they would have looked out on the blank brick wall of what would have been the end of Edmund Walter's 'Fayre House', soon to be rebuilt in 1756 as 35-37 Broad Street. In the west-facing bedroom there is evidence in a cupboard on the north wall of a window surround, which matches those in the dressing-room, but not the others in the bedroom itself; and the alteration in the floorboards suggests that the wall between the west bedroom and its dressing room may have been moved. The cornice in the dressing room is now missing on that side of the wall and a new door has at some time been inserted. Also in the dressing room, the creation of a fitted desk and wardrobe will have blocked the middle window on the first floor.

Several of the new features in the house are typical of Pritchard, and are echoed in other buildings and interiors designed by him. He came from a family of joiners, describing himself as an 'architect', and travelled widely in the area, though his work was largely confined to Shropshire and the neighbouring counties. He was closely associated with the Shrewsbury architect and surveyor, William Baker, who had been trained by Francis Smith of Warwick and was also much influenced by James Gibbs. Baker and Pritchard both worked on the Infirmary in Shrewsbury. There are many stylistic similarities in their work, for example, the use of thermal and Venetian windows, ogee arches and, above all, battlements as a Gothick ornament in, for example, Baker's work at Sibdon Castle, Shropshire, and Pritchard's battlements on Croft Castle in Herefordshire (later removed), the gazebo at 27 Broad Street, Ludlow, and the Broad Gate itself. Eighteenth-century Gothick architecture was mainly inspired by medieval churches, but castles were also a strong influence and one particularly appropriate in Ludlow.

Pritchard is known to have been working in Ludlow at an early stage in his career. In January 1744, at the age of twenty, he was paid a guinea for preparing a scheme for pulling down the medieval cross and building the

Buttercross in its place. On 2nd March 1744 he submitted his plan, which no longer exists, but it was Baker's design which was chosen. Pritchard was working on Hosyer's Almshouses in 1758 and later, in 1764, on 27 Broad Street, and in 1766 on the Guildhall and the town gaol at Galdeford. In her biography of Pritchard, Julia Ionides suggests that there was no reason why, young as he was, he could not have worked on the Broad Gate during the years 1745 to 1760 or even later, as, she says, there were still two years to run on the lease when Samuel died in 1760.[65] In fact, by the time the Stead lease ran out in 1755, Samuel Sprott had already taken on another lease which would run until 1782.[66] Mary, his widow, lived on at the house until she died in 1772 and could well have continued to employ Pritchard.

A strong reason for considering his involvement in the alterations for the Broad Gate is that Pritchard already had some connection with the Sprott family. Henry Sprott, Samuel's brother, died in 1744 and it is likely that in the following years Pritchard provided the wall monument for him in Barrow church. It also commemorates his wife, Anne, who died in 1763 and their son, Thomas, who died in 1740; and it was put up by Henry's second daughter, Dorothy Ashwood. Although it is not signed by Pritchard, it bears a strong resemblance to the monument to Samuel and his wife in Ludford church, which carries his signature. Pritchard lived and worked in Shrewsbury, but he retired to a farmhouse at Eyton-upon-Severn, not far from Much Wenlock, so he might already have been known to the Childes or the Sprotts. His elaborate monument to Sir Whitmore Acton at Acton Round church is another connection, as Sir Whitmore was related to the Childes by marriage.

Pritchard was the master of many styles. He was always ready to mix classical with Strawberry Hill Gothick, rococo, even chinoiserie styles in the same house, the same room, even the same chimney-piece. The front door at the Broad Gate is a good example. He had working for him three very skilful joiners, Nelson, van der Hagen and Swift, who made chimney-pieces and

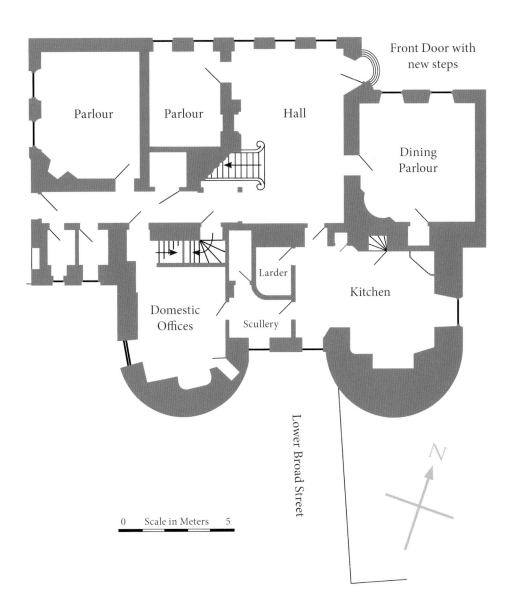

Front Door with new steps

Parlour

Parlour

Hall

Dining Parlour

Larder

Domestic Offices

Scullery

Kitchen

Lower Broad Street

N

0   Scale in Meters   5

A GROUND FLOOR PLAN OF THE SPROTT HOUSE

door-frames in all the different styles of the period. His workshop may well have supplied the Broad Gate with chimney-pieces like the beautiful rococo example at 27 Broad Street, though by the mid-twentieth century, they had, with one possible exception, been destroyed or replaced. But, although Pritchard was ready to embrace the latest fashions, he also respected the past. It is well-known that he saved Ludlow Castle by submitting a very high quotation to the government for the cost of demolition. He would have been wholly sympathetic to the desire of a client who wished to celebrate a glorious past, particularly in a building like the Broad Gate with such important medieval foundations. In a letter to the Earl of Powis in 1772 concerning a room at the Castle, he writes, 'This whole apartment has a most Elegant appearance, and shou'd be preserved to keep up the Stile and Dignity of the Old Castle'.[67] Pritchard's clients were naturally drawn to the Gothick, and he was happy to oblige them. As Julia Ionides remarks, 'Gothick could give their buildings an appearance of age and ancestry they did not always possess and thereby raise the status of the occupants'.[68] In a public building, too, like the Guildhall in Ludlow, Pritchard, while replacing the street front, was still able to echo the medieval association with the Palmers' Guild by using ogee arch windows, an ogee arch on the staircase and a Gothick door case.

The triple columns on the Guildhall door case are echoed by the staircase at Croft Castle, the garden temple at Broseley Hall, some of Pritchard's chimney-pieces and the front door surround at the Broad Gate. There are no pointed arches to the windows of the house to match the original pointed arch underneath, but it is not surprising that Pritchard kept the small-paned window in the middle of the north front, even though it serves no purpose (see Fig. 6). The entire building was rendered and cut to resemble stone. With its battlements on both sides, it would have suggested a fortified gatehouse approaching the Castle. This render is still visible on the drum towers to the south, though the battlements on that side have now been filled in. There are some remains of render on the garden front. It was also present on the north side of the house until the twentieth century. The dramatic Gothick battlements still survive, but here the render has been replaced with rough cast.

One major change to the Broad Gate which almost certainly belongs to the eighteenth century is the alteration to the line of the front elevation. The original north extension behind the drum towers would have had a continuous frontage running from east to west, with possibly as many as eleven bays centred on the arch itself.

The present arrangement is centred on the pediment, but the windows are placed in such a way that from the entrance hall, the central window looks directly from above the arch and up the middle of the street (see Fig. 15). The architect

12. THE FRONT DOOR, BROAD GATE
A mixture of styles (clustered columns and a blind fretwork chinoiserie frieze) typical of Thomas Farnolls Pritchard

could not create a conventional four-square Georgian house with rooms at each corner leading from a central hall. The structure was determined by the original passage at the back of the towers, from which a line of parlours ran along the north front. At some point, either after the fire, or more probably as part of the Sprott renovation, the eastern section, which most likely contained the original entrance, was pushed back seven feet or so (perhaps rebuilt entirely) with new larger windows and fashionable keystones over them. This allowed the room behind to be turned into a parlour with a 'best'

13. THE NORTH FRONT OF THE BROAD GATE
looking south-west. Before the mid-eighteenth century this would have continued in a straight line with windows to either end

chamber above looking out onto the street. The parlour over the arch itself was extended back into the staircase area to create a large and impressive entrance hall, which displayed the fine oak staircase to advantage.

The new front door was ingeniously placed in the angle of the two walls, with a grand semi-circular flight of stone steps leading up to it. The date of the four windows at the east end, the design of the front door, and the imaginative placing of the battlements, which have been described as climbing 'insouciantly' across the frontage and round the right angle, suggest that Pritchard had a hand in the new design.[69] The stepped battlements over the central pediment echo those on the gazebo at 27 Broad Street, and the original battlements provided by Pritchard for the south front of Croft Castle.[70] All of this would have emphasised the medieval roots of the Sprott family.

14. BATTLEMENTS ON THE GAZEBO AT 27 BROAD STREET
Designed by Thomas Farnolls Pritchard

15. *A VIEW OF THE BUTTERCROSS AND BROAD STREET*
seen from the central window of the entrance hall

– 3 –

THE SPROTTS II

Samuel Sprott appears to have been very conscious of his family's standing in society. Henry Sprott, his brother, had died in 1744 leaving no immediate male heir, as his only son, Thomas, had died young in 1740. Samuel's late marriage, after the death of his nephew and just before that of his brother, suggests that he felt a responsibility to continue an illustrious line and to keep alive the family name. It is interesting that the decorative lead panel or *cartouche* on the front of the house contains his initials alone and not those of his wife, as would have been normal in a marriage panel; it might, of course, have been placed there as a pious tribute by his widow. The frontage of his house, situated in such a prominent position at the focal point of the most important street in the town, now made an imposing statement about his social rank.

Samuel was certainly much admired by his aunt Anne, widow of John Pryce DD, Rector of Westbury, near Shrewsbury. As we have seen (on p. 51), she had a mind of her own. She suffered the double tragedy of losing her husband and, soon after, seeing her house burn down with his will in it.[71] In her own will of 1748, she left to 'my much beloved nephew Samuel Sprott, Dr of Physick... if he acts as executor, £8 to buy mourning'. She also left to him 'the largest silver coffee pot, the great Salt which I lent my sister Sprott (his

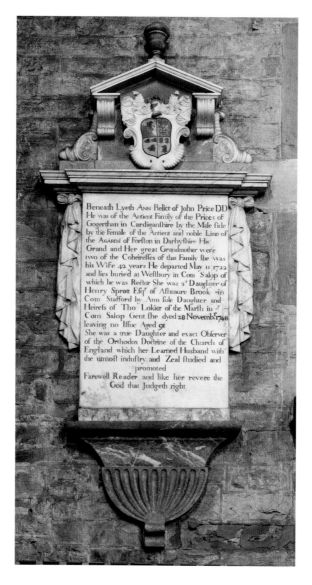

Beneath Lyeth Ann Relict of John Price DD
He was of the Antient Family of the Prices of
Gogerthan in Cardiganshire by the Male side
by the Female of the Antient and noble Line of
the Agards of Forston in Darbyshire His
Grand and Her great Grandmother were
two of the Coheiresses of that Family she was
his Wife 42 years He departed May 11 1722
and lies buried at Westbury in Com Salop of
which he was Rector She was 2ᵈ Daughter of
Henry Sprott Esqʳ of Ashmore Brook in
Com Stafford by Ann sole Daughter and
Heiress of Tho Lokier of the Marsh in
Com Salop Gent she dyed 28 Novembʳ 1748
leaving no Issue Aged 91
She was a true Daughter and exact Observer
of the Orthodox Doctrine of the Church of
England which her Learned Husband with
the utmost industry and Zeal studied and
promoted
Farewell Reader and like her revere the
God that Judgeth right

16. MEMORIAL TO ANNE PRYCE

mother) and is now in Broad Gate House, all my books and pamphlets and written manuscripts, pedigree of the very ancient family of the Agards', and a 'picture of myself to be hanged near his own'. Her impressive memorial tablet, which is placed in St John's chapel in St Laurence's church, Ludlow, to

17. THE LEAD PANEL ON THE FRONT OF THE NORTH-FACING PEDIMENT
with entwined double Ss for Samuel Sprott

the left of the Palmers' Guild window, emphasises her (and her husband's) descent from the Agards. Part of the very long inscription on it reads:

> *Beneath Lyeth Ann Relict of John Price DD*
> *He was of the Antient family of the Prices of*
> *Gogerthan in Cardiganshire by the Male side*
> *by the Female of the Antient and noble Line of*
> *the AGARDS of Forston in Darbyshire His*
> *Grand and her great Grandmother were*
> *two of the Coheiresses of that family she was*
> *his Wife 42 years He departed May 11 1722*
> *and lies buried at Westbury in Com Salop of*
> *which he was Rector She was 2d Daughter of*
> *Henry Sprott Esqr of Ashmore Brook in*
> *Com Stafford by Ann sole Daughter and*
> *Heiress of Tho Lokier of the Marsh in*
> *Com Salop Gent she dyed 28 Novembr 1748*
> *leaving no issue Aged 91*

65

This reinforces the impression that the family was very conscious of its origins. Not only had they married into the Lockier family, and had the distinction of a royalist ancestor, Edward Sprott, who, as Captain of Foot under the Earl of Chesterfield, was killed at the Battle of Marston Moor, but they were also connected to one of the most important of Midland families, the Agards of Foston Hall in Derbyshire, who had possessions in Ireland as well. William Agard was the nephew of the celebrated Elizabethan archivist and antiquarian, Arthur Agard (1536-1615). William had married Mabel, daughter of Francis Agard of Dublin, and it was their daughter, Mary, who married Thomas Sprott of Ashmore Brook, Lichfield. Her brother, Sir Henry Agard (1581-1635), was knighted in 1617. Anne Pryce's memorial tablet, accordingly, is adorned with a quartered shield bearing the coats of arms of the Sprotts, the Pryces, the Lockiers and the Agards. With this pedigree Samuel Sprott had every reason to be proud of his lineage. Looking from his ancient drum towers and Gothick battlements up the hill into the town and out into the countryside around, he could be very pleased with his own castle.

It seems likely that in spite of being very well endowed with land and property in Staffordshire and Shropshire, Dr Sprott actively practised medicine in Ludlow, probably from the house itself. Indeed, the attraction of the Broad Gate might have been that under John Stead it was already the home of a thriving medical practice. Like John Stead before him, Samuel Sprott was described as a physician. That should have meant that they had studied theoretical medicine in Oxford, Cambridge, one of the Scottish universities, or on the continent, and that they came, as was usual, from the middle or professional classes, or above. Samuel himself, 'son of Thomas Sprott of Barrow, Salop, armiger', had matriculated when he was eighteen at Christ Church, Oxford in 1715, where his father and brother had also studied, and graduated as Bachelor of Medicine in 1729.[72] Surgeons, or surgeon-apothecaries, originally were of a lower social status and were apprenticed to members of the family or to friends in what was thought of as a trade rather than a profession. They were involved in the manual labour of the more brutal side of medicine – tooth-drawing, amputations and other surgical operations, whereas it was assumed that physicians, who were distinguished by their intellect and education, hardly touched their patients, except perhaps to take their pulse, and never got their hands dirty. They read symptoms, diagnosed illnesses and prescribed medicines, which would be made up for them by pharmacists.

The eighteenth century, however, was a time of great change in the practice of medicine. With major advances in anatomy and midwifery, the authority and social status of surgeons rose, so that there was often some confusion about their position in society. John Stead himself was at first described as an 'apothecary' and later as 'Doctor of Physick'. Surgeons, who were apothecaries and often men-midwives as well, were not allowed to charge for consultations, so their income often came from the sale of medicines in their apothecaries' shops. They were an essential aid to the poorer part of society. Physicians were generally suspicious of their influence, and strenuously maintained the difference:

> The sick call the apothecary "doctor". If allowed to do so they will soon think him a fit and lawful practitioner.[73]

It is true that surgeons were 'not of an Academical but Mechanick education', but many were self-educated and in the forefront of scientific exploration in the late seventeenth and early eighteenth century. In *The London Tradesman* (1747) R. Campbell heaps praise on them:

> The Surgeon is the second branch of the medical art, very little inferior to the first in point of utility, but founded upon principles much more certain, and less precarious … The Physician … is frequently obliged to grope in the dark, to act by guess and bare conjecture, and depends more upon chance and the strength of the patient's constitution,

than upon any infallible rules in his art; but the Surgeon ... has the evidence of his senses, as well as his judgment ... His method of cure depends upon the known mechanism of the human system, and the medicines he uses act by known laws, established by a long course of experience ... The genius of Surgeons differs very little from that required in a Physician. To a solid judgment, quick apprehension and a good memory, he must add a kind of courage peculiar to himself ... [He must have] a lion's heart, a hawk's eye and a lady's hand.[74]

The surgeons themselves worked hard at this period to to achieve regulation and recognition. They separated themselves from the barbers and very often seem to have taken out episcopal licences to practise as physicians later in their careers. This accounts perhaps for the change in the elder John Stead's titles, and for the general blurring of distinctions.

A good illustration of this change is provided by the Navy's surgeons, who originally occupied a middle rank in the wardroom, but by the early years of the nineteenth century were required to wear a Captain's undress uniform with stand-up collar. Physicians, though, were still allowed gold lace on their sleeves to distinguish them.[75] The distinction, however, was becoming increasingly irrelevant. When Thomas Lloyd, who, as we shall see, grew up at the Broad Gate, became a doctor in the 1820s, he studied anatomy with surgeons in Bristol in 1822, and took his degree at Edinburgh in 1826. His first post was as an assistant surgeon in Bombay for three years, but when he returned to Ludlow it was as Senior Physician at the Ludlow Dispensary. Even today, when surgeons are often regarded as the aristocrats of the medical profession, their basic training is the same as that for physicians, although they are addressed as plain 'Mr', while physicians are 'Doctor'.

Doctors Stead and Sprott, whether as surgeons or physicians, would have been trained in the medical theory of the early eighteenth century. In spite of advances such as the discovery of the circulation of the blood, the use of the thermometer and the introduction of chemical medicines, that theory was still based on the medieval idea of the four humours (represented by black and yellow bile, phlegm and blood), and treatment was still aimed at rectifying the balance of these in the body by the expulsion of excessive substances. This involved purging, vomiting, blistering, sweating or bleeding. Bleeding was induced by the use of leeches or the practice of 'cupping' to bring blood to the surface, where it could be let out. A great many of the medicines prescribed were still based on plants and herbs, and the introduction of chemicals, unfortunately, involved the widespread use of lead and mercury. Treatment seems to have been based on trial and error, kill or cure.

As with the changes in consumption generally, medicine was a profitable market, and patent cures and proprietary medicines proliferated. Doctor Askew's pills or Dr Radcliffe's Elixir might be widely advertised and recommended, and could make fortunes for practitioners; and, of course, there were many quacks and impostors. Even a very reputable physician in the eighteenth century like Dr William Cullen, who became Professor of Medicine at Glasgow University and was in many ways ahead of his time, used in his medicines such ingredients as lead oxide, carabid beetles, whisky, arsenic, quicklime, hemlock, mercury, rum, tin, woodlice, Epsom salts, garlic, ginseng and woman's milk, as well as such herbs and plants as nicotiana, nutmeg, parsley, peppermint, rosemary, St John's wort and valerian. His only analgesic was laudanum, liquid opium mixed with alcohol, which was addictive.[76]

Doctors at this time practised from home with, perhaps, a male assistant or apprentice. They did their rounds on horseback or carriage in all weathers and, if they were good men, they adjusted their fees to help poorer people, who were turning increasingly to them. Although their patients were mainly of the middle and upper classes, the dispensary in Ludlow, supported by subscription, gave 'medical assistance and medicines *gratis* to inhabitants of the town in indigent circumstances'. The mid-eighteenth century also saw the rise of benefit societies where people could save towards their medical fees. By 1810, there was a charitable society in Ludlow for the relief of lying-in women, but only if they were married and of good character.[77] On the whole, doctors prospered, particularly in the second half of the eighteenth century, when they had high professional status; their clientèle expanded, and there were important new advances such as inoculation against smallpox.

Samuel Sprott practised medicine in and around Ludlow. His brother-in-law, Henry Jordan, was an apothecary living in Lower Galdeford, and they may have worked together. We also know that Samuel left money in his will for his young servant to be apprenticed, no doubt as an apothecary or surgeon. This would not have prevented him and his wife from taking part in the social life of the town, and, given their connections, among the highest circles. Apparently, they had no children. There is a record of a 'Mary Stott', born to Samuel and Mary Stott in the Ludlow Parish Register. She was baptized on 27th May 1748, but nothing more is known of her. It might be thought that the William Sprott who married Samuel's niece, Joyce Yate, was his son, but there is no record of his birth in Ludlow, and, since Joyce Yate's marriage took place in 1755, when a son of Samuel and Mary could not have been older than ten or eleven, this seems very unlikely. Joyce, who was the daughter of Samuel's sister, Anne, and John Yate, Gent. of Ashford Carbonel, did indeed marry a William Sprott from Leominster at Ludford church on 23rd October 1755, and, according to the Easter books, the couple lived in Ludlow. This William eventually died and was buried in Ludlow in 1792. He may have been the William Sprott who appears in the Corporation Minutes for November 1781 as one of three individuals seeking to become free burgesses of the borough, but 'refused by the Corporation'.[78] He is described there as William Sprott, of Ashford, Gent. but he is not mentioned in any of the Sprott wills. Was he a distant relation, or a black sheep in the family? What, one wonders, had he done to be rejected by the Corporation?

Lacking any immediate male heirs, Samuel Sprott willed that, after his wife's death, his property should go to Thomas Porter Ashwood, the son of his niece Dorothy, the second of Henry Sprott's three daughters. But Thomas died aged nineteen while still a student at Oriel College Oxford, before he could inherit, and the estate eventually passed to Thomas Yate of Ashford Carbonel, the son of Samuel's youngest sister, Anne, and brother of the younger Joyce. Samuel himself died in 1760, although his will was drawn up in 1753. Even though some of the estate was entailed, he was able to leave to his wife, Mary, for her lifetime, 'all lands including the capital messuage called The Marsh [which by this time he had inherited from his brother]; to his servant, Richard Kendrick, £10 to place him apprentice; [and] to his wife the tenement where I now live . . . and [the] tenement adjoining[the cottage fronting the western tower] for her life'. There were various monetary gifts to Samuel's sisters, nieces and great-nieces. 'All his goods, chattels and personal estate' were left to his widow, who was his executrix. Later, 23, Broad Street, a freehold property belonging to the Sprotts, was left to Samuel's nephew, Henry Yate, in 1788, and the Marsh was bequeathed by Thomas Yate to his cousin, Mrs Elizabeth Toldervy. She left it to Yate's son, Samuel Yate Sprott, who left it to another cousin's son, William Moseley, who sold it.

In November 1760 Samuel Sprott was buried at Ludford Church. He was, at first, commemorated by a memorial tablet in the Fox chapel, reading simply, 'Here lyeth the body of Samuel SPROTT who Died November the 24th 1760 aged 63', with crossed bones on each corner and no other decoration.[79] After his wife's death in 1772, it was thought by either the Sprotts or the Childes that there should be a more elaborate memorial to them both, and another tablet was placed in a conspicuous position on the west wall of the church. It is very like the memorial to his brother, Henry, in Barrow church, with the same use of contrasting marble. It has an urn at the top, crossed bones on each corner, and a *cartouche* at the bottom, flanked by upturned palm fronds. On one side at the front is Pritchard's name,

18. MEMORIALS DESIGNED BY PRITCHARD
to Henry Sprott, d. 1744, in Barrow Church, and to Samuel Sprott, d. 1760, in Ludford Church

with its characteristic alignment of the T and F, and on the other 'Salop. Arct.'. It is worth remarking that while the size and shape of the memorial to Samuel and Mary Sprott are almost identical to those of the memorial to Henry (with his wife and son) in Barrow church, Henry's inscription is expressed in English, his wife and son are given equal prominence and the *cartouche* below is left blank. On the Ludford memorial, by contrast, the inscription is in Latin and emphasises Mary's connection with a titled family. The shield painted on the *cartouche* is impaled with both the Sprott coat of arms and that of the Childe family, and it is only Samuel's name that has been engraved in capital letters:

Iuxta Jacent Reliquiae
SAMUELIS SPROTT
de la Marsh in Com Salop M.B.
Uxorem duxit
Mariam filiam Thomae Child
de Birch in eodem Com Arm.
Ille obijt 24.° Nov.ˢ 1760
Ætat. 64.
Illa 18.° Jan: 1772.°
Ætat. 66.°

In Mary's will, drawn up in 1769, the terms of the marriage settlement of 1745 are repeated, referring to the extensive lands in Staffordshire, Shropshire and the City of Lichfield. Most of the unentailed part of the estate went to two of her nieces, Elizabeth Toldervy and Dorothy Ashwood, both daughters of Samuel's brother Henry, and to their mother, her sister Anne.

After Mary's death, the Broad Gate seems to have been sublet, first to a Captain Poole (who was probably a relative of the Rev. Poole, curate of Ludford) who paid the window tax in 1773 and 1774, and then to a Mrs Congreve who paid the window tax in 1775 and 1776 and the Poor Rate from 1777 to 1779. She has not been identified with any certainty, but the monumental inscriptions in St Giles's Church, Ludford, include one to Anna Catherine Congreve, who died on June 24th 1779, aged sixty-one. Her daughter, Charlotte, who died in 1795, is also commemorated. The only event worth recording in Mrs Congreve's time at the house is an earthquake on 8th September 1775, mentioned by the painter, Thomas Jones, and felt as far away as Bristol.[80] It could account for the lack of alignment in the cornice in the drawing room at the west end of the building.

Thomas Porter Ashwood, grandson of his brother, Henry, would have been Samuel's nearest male relative and, had he not died in 1767, he would have inherited Samuel's estate when Mary Sprott died. As his executrix, it was Thomas's mother, Dorothy Ashwood, who took out a new lease on the Broad Gate from the Corporation in 1782.[81] Here she is described as 'widow, exec. of Thomas Porter Ashwood, her late son … who was devisee [heir] of Samuel Sprott, Bachelor of Physick'. She was to pay 32s for the 'messuage/ tenement with court before the same/stables/garden adjoining over and adjoining the Broad Gate', and 10s rent for the 'messuage/tenement/garden/ Town Ditch … adjacent to Broad Gate on west side'. She did not live at the Broad Gate as she had her own house at 39 Broad Street. When she died in the following year, 1783, her personal property was left to her daughter and family, and the entailed estates of the Sprotts went to the nearest male heir in the family, her cousin Thomas Yate of Ashford Carbonel. To keep the family's name alive, Thomas Yate's son, Samuel, who inherited from his father in 1797, changed his name to Samuel Yate Sprott by letters patent that year, and, with the Sprott money, built Ashford Court. He married Lucy Oakley in 1801, but they had no children, and he died later that year. When she inherited the lease, his wife preferred to stay in Ashford Carbonel rather than take over the Broad Gate, and so the house passed from the Sprotts.

– 4 –

SOCIAL LIFE IN
EIGHTEENTH CENTURY LUDLOW

In late August 1771 Mrs Lybbe Powys, her husband and small son set off from their home in Oxfordshire to spend three weeks with their relatives, the Hills, at Court of Hill near Nash, about ten miles from Ludlow. They were great travellers and she recorded their many journeys around the country in journals and letters which give a full and vivid account of the places they visited. Their arrival at Court of Hill coincided with one of Ludlow's 'seasons' and they were able to go to the races, the special balls and parties in the town and the theatre in Mill Street, as well as travelling round to dine with the local families, like the Blounts at Mawley Hall, and their Powys relations at Henley Hall.[82] Mrs Lybbe Powys's husband, Philip Lybbe Powys, was elected an absentee burgess of Ludlow Corporation in 1782.

The Season varied very much between London and the country, between spa towns and provincial cities, and between large towns and small. In London, it coincided with the Parliamentary sessions, legal terms and the presence of the royal family and court. The Hills of Court of Hill spent the whole winter in London, as Thomas Hill was an MP. The Season at Bath lasted the whole summer and, in later years, most of the winter, but in market towns like Ludlow the seasons were much shorter and coincided

19. COURT OF HILL, NEAR LUDLOW
Home of Sir Thomas Hill and his family, visited by Mrs Lybbe Powys with her husband and son
in 1771, which would have been well-known to Lucy Maria Kinnersley

with the local elections, the assizes, race meetings and associated balls and entertainments. The most important balls were the Bailiffs' balls, held on the occasion of the exchange of Bailiffs by the Corporation in late October.

To be a successful magnet for tourists, a town needed, apart from good accommodation, a nearby race course, assembly rooms for balls and receptions, venues for concerts, a theatre for entertainment and pleasant walks where the fashionable could see and be seen. If possible it should also have medicinal waters. In his 1812 *Description of the Town of Ludlow*, William Felton, the printer, mentions the Saltmore well in a meadow to the east of Ludlow, which he considers could have been developed as a spa. By 1826, Thomas Wright (father of Thomas Wright the antiquarian) wrote that 'great benefit has been found to arise from the free use of this water,' and that 'accommodations are now completed at the cottage [nearby] for cold or warm bathing', but in the eighteenth century, apart from the ancient spring or 'boiling well' in the meadows by the Corve, and the 'sugar well', 'noted for its sweet taste and healing qualities', Ludlow had no curative waters.[83] By the 1770s, however, it had everything else it needed to attract visitors.

The Castle had for centuries been the centre for cultural and social activities. It still retained a bowling green and fives court, but the last ball held there was in 1719, and Defoe describes it in 1725 as a ruin.[84] Once it had been abandoned, there was a need for a proper assembly room. Some inns had rooms for entertainment, but something larger was required and the 'long room' at the market house, which had been built in 1706 to replace an earlier Tudor building, was adapted to provide a social space. The Corporation Minutes reveal that the walls and ceiling were boarded and the walls panelled with walnut by 1724, paid for by Henry Herbert of Oakly Park, no doubt to ingratiate himself with the electorate. Fine chandeliers were ordered in 1774, 'one with twelve sconces and the other two eight each', and in 1775 Mr Ralph Thomas was paid £47.5.0 for 'Three Elegant Chandeliers' for the Market House. Four new sash windows were installed on the south side of the Long Room by 1786.

There had been a terrace walk on the north side of the churchyard since at least 1694; and before 1747 the Castle Ditch at Dinham had been turned into a new walk, as can be seen in the Vogelsanck panorama and in a panel painting at the Broad Gate. In 1771 the Countess of Powis had a promenade laid out round the Castle with rails and gates. It was later planted with trees and called the 'Mall'. For entertainment, strolling players had always performed at the inns, but by 1770 there was a proper theatre in Mill Street, at which Mrs Siddons later acted, and concerts were held in the church. There was a race course, originally in the Linney fields to the west of the town, but by 1739 moved to its present site at Bromfield. Horse races were first recorded in 1725. Sixteen meetings a year were held by 1728 and racing soon became an annual three-day event, followed each evening by a ball. This was the occasion which the Lybbe Powyses and their relations were attending.

Ludlow was well-known for good accommodation, cheap food, fine air and water; and it was surrounded by a network of landed families connected closely by marriage and property, for whom the town was a natural centre. All of this was good for the business of the succession of doctors and lawyers who lived at the Broad Gate. According to *The Modern Universal British Traveller* (1779), 'Ludlow is a large, populous town … the houses are well built, the streets exceeding clean and many people of rank and fortune constantly reside in it'.[85] Visitors also arrived from the wider world, bringing with them new fashions and experience of a more sophisticated culture than was usually available in the provinces. Traditional town customs and entertainments, such as the violent 'rope-pulling' (tug of war) which took place every Shrove Tuesday, and the circuses, boxing, ratting and cock-fighting, were now left to the lower classes. Instead, a more outward-looking culture, reinforced by newspapers and lending libraries, with plays and music emanating from the metropolis, was reflected in the abandonment of local vernacular architecture, and the embracing of the more cosmopolitan classical style in building. This London-centred culture was one to which the more educated and prosperous minor gentry and even a growing class of successful tradesmen, could aspire. It was reflected in the increase in specialist dealers in books and luxury goods who appeared in the town at this period, and in the growth of private educational establishments and clubs, which met in inns and coffee houses and fed an increasing appetite for self-improvement. Ludlow was known for its urbanity. Philip Luckombe in 1764 declared that 'the inhabitants are reckoned more polite than their neighbours'.[86]

The Hills took lodgings for themselves and their guests in Ludlow for the races and the ball that followed, but many prosperous families could afford to buy or rent a house in town as well as in the country and used Ludlow as their winter quarters. Lord and Lady Powis, the Boynes of Burwarton, the Dunnes of Gatley Court, the Pearces of Downton Hall and the Salweys of Richard's Castle were among many local families who, like the Sprotts, bought or inherited houses in Broad Street, though, unlike them, Samuel Sprott did not occupy his country estate. He had inherited the Marsh from his brother Henry, but his sister-in-law may have continued to live there, and, when he practised as a physician, he would have needed to reside in the town for most of the time. County families normally regarded their country 'seat' as their most important residence. The land was usually their main source of income and they needed to be around for the harvests, the hunting season and family gatherings at Christmas. The town, however, was essential for business, for politics, for company, for shopping and, most importantly, for the disposing of their sons and daughters in marriage.

In the winter, despite the new turnpike trusts of 1751 and 1756, the local country roads were often impassable. On an expedition to see Sir Thomas Hill's lime kilns on Clee Hill (which she describes as 'a vast mountain') Mrs Lybbe Powys records the traveller's difficulties in the area:

> *The roads about here are wonderful to strangers. Where they are mending, as they call it, you travel over a bed of loose stones, none of less size than an octavo volume; and where not mended 'tis like a staircase … they appear unfit for ladies travelling, but they mind them not … As to carriages, they make nothing of going a dozen miles to dinner, tho' own to being bruised to death, and quite* deshabbiller'd *by jolts they must receive.*[87]

While the elegant houses and greater convenience of Ludlow offered the gentry more comfort, especially in the winter, the town also provided them with better opportunities for meeting friends and relations and also for enlarging their circle of acquaintance and giving their young people more choice during the social season in finding husbands or wives. These serious matters were still largely arranged by parents, but the young were increasingly allowed to have the last word. Even with a house full of guests, life in the country itself was often not particularly exciting.

According to Mrs Lybbe Powys:

Sunday passed as usual, with people cheerfully thanking for the enjoyments of life. Monday, the morning, as usual, divided into parties of riding, walking, shooting, reading, working [needlework], drawing. Never met at dinner till after four … though, indeed, in the shooting season seldom before five. A walk in general after tea, and in the evening, a large pope [card] table, another quadrille and many lookers-on besides; never supp'd till near eleven or abed till near two.[88]

It must have seemed much more glamorous for the young people to mix at the Assemblies with the best society in the county, in the hope of seeing some new faces. The writer and spy, John Macky, wrote in 1722:

formerly the country ladies were stewed up in their fathers' old mansion houses, and seldom saw company but at an assize, a horse-race, or a fair, but by means of these assemblies, matches are struck up and the officers of the army have had pretty good success where ladies are at their own disposal.[89]

In spite of this, marriages tended to be within the same narrow social group and, as with the Sprotts and, later, the Lloyds, there are many instances of brothers and sisters marrying into the same family, or allying themselves with neighbours or families to whom they were already related. Mrs Lybbe Powys makes quite a joke of this:

There seems such confusion with the intermarriages of our cousins, that I give over recollecting who they were, and rest satisfied with who they are. Mr Hill married a Miss Rock, and Mr Rock a Miss Hill &c., &c., just at the same period; so that, as a smart gentleman said on paying the wedding visits, 'Really, the Rocks having turn'ed into Hills, and the Hills into Rocks, it was utterly impossible to distinguish them so as to pay each of them his proper compliments on the occasion'.[91]

There was always the possibility, though, of a girl from a less aristocratic background marrying into a higher social class, as in the case of Harriet Baugh, daughter of the Ludlow Town Clerk. In 1796 she married Gustavus Hamilton, a young army officer, who in 1826 became the sixth Viscount Boyne. It was not exactly a Cinderella story, though, as she had inherited the Burwarton estate through her mother, and, according to Mary Sneade, her fortune was the object.[92]

The Lybbe Powyses' party left Court of Hill on Thursday, 4th September, 1771 for the races, and stayed in Ludlow until Saturday. Like the Pardoes, cousins of the Hills, they lodged at the Salweys' house, 52 Broad Street. Mrs Lybbe Powys describes the race course, which she much admired, and gives an account of the ball at the old assembly rooms in the evening:

We got to the ball about nine, a very agreeable one, tho' 'twas said not near so brilliant as formerly. This, indeed, I can easily conceive by our race-assembly at Reading, which used to be thought next to York; but the fashionable resort to water-drinking places every summer takes from each county those young people who otherwise would be ambitious of shining at these annual balls. However, Ludlow's assembly, with two lords and six baronets' families, might be stil'd tolerable, tho' it seem'd a mortifying thing that Lord Clive's family were at Spaw [the spa], and Lady Powys ill in London. Mr. Conyngham and Greenly, as stewards, were, of course, masters of the ceremony, assisted by their ladies. Mrs. Conyngham must be ever most elegant, but such a figure ornamented by dress and jewels must be still more conspicuous. There were many pretty women – Miss Pardoe greatly admired ... a very fine girl, all pleasing vivacity.[92]

This is Lucy Maria Pardoe, who was later to live at the Broad Gate after her marriage to James Kinnersley (see p. 87).

The Hills' party adjourned to Mr Pardoe's, where they had supper and were 'not abed as you may suppose till near five'. The next day was taken up with a visit to the theatre, another expedition to the races, followed by a dinner for the ladies at Mr Davies's house, 27 Broad Street, another assembly and an all-night supper at the Hill's lodgings. They returned to Court of Hill the following day, but not before Mrs Lybbe Powys had time to walk around Ludlow, which she describes as 'the prettiest town in England'.

The appearance of the town was changing, not just in its adoption of the Georgian style in domestic architecture, but in alterations to public buildings and general amenities. With the help of Baker and Pritchard, in 1743-4 the old medieval cross had been replaced by the fine new Buttercross; Hosyer's Almshouses were rebuilt with the town's coat of arms in the pediment in 1758; and the Guildhall refaced in a fashionable Gothick style in 1766. To diminish the general filth and mud, and the presence of animals, the shambles at the top of Mill Street had been moved. There had been a problem with pigs running wild in the streets, but in 1744 the Corporation determined to remove them. The 'heaps of dirt' which John Stead had agreed to deal with in 1686 were no longer so much in evidence. There was new paving in the streets and oil-burning lamps to light them; there were public conduits and, for those who paid for it, even piped water, though it was best to have one's own spring or well as the water pumped from the river was polluted with sewage. By the end of the century, Burfoot and Wilkes's *Universal Directory* was reporting that there were 'four conduits supplied with spring water, and a river engine which fills a reservoir from which water is conveyed to any house'.[93]

Communications with the outside world had also greatly improved. By 1763 there was a stage coach service to and from London and the new turnpike roads made travel much less tedious. There was more emphasis on domestic comfort, too, and a desire for acquiring new possessions which was satisfied by the arrival of new kinds of shops selling furniture, ornaments or 'toys', musical instruments, clocks and watches, china, wigs, tea, chocolate and coffee, and the new, practical fabrics, such as muslin and chintz. This all encouraged social intercourse and visits to other people's houses. As an anonymous visitor to Ludlow in 1744 remarked, 'here the gentry dress fine, live easily, visit much and do things very grand'.[94]

By the 1790s the social scene had not much changed. In her book, *Ayot Rectory*, Carola Oman reconstructs the lives of the Sneade daughters at this period in Ludlow. The three Sneade girls, Elizabeth, Mary and Ellen, lived much of the year at Brand House in Brand Lane (the very house that John Stead had built around 1684), though their father was Rector of Bedstone and they returned there for the summer. The Rev. Samuel Sneade justified his absence from his parish by saying that he and his wife 'lived in Ludlow for the advantages of education and society for their three daughters'.[95] Mary, the second daughter, married a London merchant, Joseph Brown, and her daughter, Ellen Olive, left materials for a memoir of her mother's life in two manuscript volumes and an assortment of notes and letters which came to Carola Oman and from which she wrote her book. The first part is an account of the various courtships of the sisters and of their rejected suitors, and the round of parties, balls and receptions they attended:

Ludlow was at this time a pleasant residence, not only on account of its unequalled natural beauty and noble historical monuments, but because of the company to be met there. Several Irish families of consequence had arrived to escape the revolutionary terrors of their own country … and [also] French refugees of high degree … Hours were earlier in Ludlow than in London, dress was simpler and repasts were less elaborate. Mary Sneade loved to tell her own daughters of the pure fun and frivolity of her first Ludlow season – Broad Street gay with rapid feet and glancing eyes; the shopping expeditions for tomorrow's ball; the little encounters with partners from last night's ball – scarlet coats and blue and black (sons of neighbours who had taken up the family living)...There were at this time two principal seasons of gaiety in Ludlow. The summer races were attended by a ball and a summer breakfast on the Castle Green. In the winter there were the Bailiff's balls in the old tumbledown Assembly Rooms, and more private dances.[96]

One highlight of the summer of 1802 was the visit to Ludlow of Admiral Horatio Nelson with Sir William and Lady Hamilton. Mrs Stackhouse Acton, the niece of Richard Payne Knight, recalled seeing them:

I have a recollection of being held up in my nurse's arms to see Lord Nelson at an open window at the Crown Inn at Ludlow with another gentleman and a lady, who I suppose were Sir William and Lady Hamilton. They were on their way to visit my uncle at Downton Castle.[97]

Nelson was elected an honorary burgess of the Corporation and a reception was held in his honour, but, because of the nature of his relationship with Lady Hamilton, the Sneade girls were not allowed to attend. There may have already been a connection with the Nelson family, for Nelson's elder brother, the Rev. William Nelson, was an absentee burgess from 1795, and his nephew-in-law, Samuel Hood, who had married the admiral's niece, Charlotte, was elected in 1810.

Another distinguished visitor was Lucien Bonaparte, brother of Napoleon, captured while on his way to America, and taken with his family into exile in this country. He lived for a short time at Dinham House and attended a ball in 1811. While some of his family danced, he spent his time in the card room. He is described as 'a man of considerable talent', with an extensive and magnificent collection of prints and drawings, and as a lover of music, having 'frequent concerts of vocal and instrumental music'. He would have been a great asset to Ludlow had he stayed longer.[98]

Among the neighbours known to the Sneades we find Dr William Moseley, the son of Samuel Sprott's niece, Anne. Other acquaintances included the

20. NASH COURT, NEAR LUDLOW
Home of the Pardoe family, where Lucy Maria Kinnersley grew up

Pardoes of Nash Court, who appear in Mrs Lybbe Powys's account. Their son, George Dansey Pardoe, was courting Ellen Sneade, the youngest Sneade daughter. He was the nephew and later executor of Lucy Maria Kinnersley. Although he came from a good family, as Carola Oman recounts:

> *it was not a connexion desired by the parents. Although he was most gentleman-like and had the estate of Nash … it was encumbered and his character was unfitted to the ministry which he had been led to enter to increase his income to enable him to marry. Ellen, however, was determined 'to have her George and a crust' and objections were fruitless.*[99]

It was impossible then for a young man to marry and support a wife, children and a household of servants, as would be expected, without a secure income. The consequence was that women often had long engagements and were married late, frequently to much older men, for security and status. The history of the Broad Gate itself contains two such examples, one of them George Pardoe's aunt, Lucy.

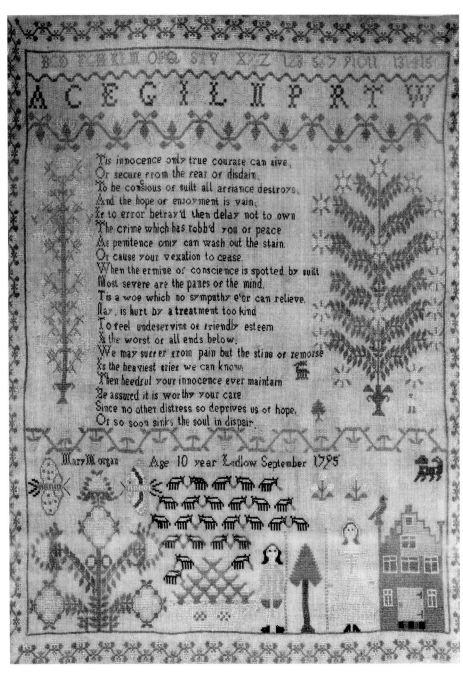

21. A SAMPLER CREATED IN LUDLOW IN 1795 BY MARY MORGAN AGED TEN
showing a battlemented house almost certainly based on the Broad Gate

− 5 −

THE KINNERSLEYS
1785-1814

By 1784 James Kinnersley had appeared in the story of the Broad Gate. He would have been well-known to the Sprotts, since as an attorney he had witnessed a codicil to Mary Sprott's will in 1771, acted as trustee for her niece Joyce Sprott's will in 1797, and witnessed Dorothy Ashwood's will in 1782. He and his son also had connections with the Lloyds of Weobley, who later lived at the Broad Gate, so he is a bridge between the two families. He came from an old Herefordshire family and was the son of George and Jane Kinnersley, who lived at the Lynch, later Lynch Court, outside Eardisland. His first wife, Anne, died in 1764, leaving at least two sons: Richard, who matriculated at Brasenose College, Oxford, in January 1769 aged seventeen, but predeceased his father in 1786 aged thirty-five, and a second son, James. In 1784 James Kinnersley the elder married, as his second wife, Lucy Maria Pardoe, that 'very fine girl, all pleasing vivacity' of whom we have heard in Mrs Lybbe Powys's journal. She was the sister of George Pardoe, who lived with his wife Ellen, neé Dansey, at Nash Court with a large and thriving family, and she was the aunt of George Dansey Pardoe, who was at last allowed to marry Ellen Sneade on November 24th 1809. The Pardoes were, again, like the Sprotts, intimately connected by marriage to all the local gentry, including the more aristocratic Lacon and Childe families. James and Lucy Kinnersley had no children, but the youngest of Lucy's nephews, born in 1791, took the name James Kinnersley Pardoe. By 1785 James and Lucy Kinnersley were living at the Broad Gate. The *Easter Book* for that year records 'Mr Kinnersley, attorney', and his wife at the house. In 1788 James's widowed mother-in-law, Mrs Pardoe, and her maid were lodging with them.

James Kinnersley the elder was an important figure in Ludlow. He was a lawyer and one of the first bankers in the town, and was frequently cited as a witness or trustee or arbiter. When he was elected a burgess by Ludlow Corporation in 1784, his 'certificate' made clear that this was as a result of his marriage to Lucy Pardoe, her deceased father, George Pardoe, having been a burgess. He was familiar with the important men in South Shropshire and North Herefordshire. On 3rd January 1792 he corresponded with Richard Payne Knight MP over the Ludlow election, and he was on friendly terms with Thomas Johnes of Croft Castle. In September 1794 he subscribed to a history of Ludlow Castle. This is likely to have been *An Historical Account of Ludlow Castle*, by William Hodges, published by William Felton, rather than *The History of Ludlow Castle* by John Thomas, published in the same year, which bankrupted its author because there were over three hundred subscriptions for the other book.

James Kinnersley's own financial affairs seem to have been very disorganised for a banker. According to the Easter book for 1798, thirteen payments of church dues were outstanding, and his estate was later found to be encumbered with debt. He was also rather relaxed as a lawyer. He received letters addressed to him as simply 'James Kinnersley Esq., attorney at law, Ludlow, Salop', so he was clearly very well known. One letter, from Matthew Bright of Bristol in 1797, treats him with great respect:

We shall always pay attention to the recommendation of a Gentleman whose reputation stands so high as J. Kinnersley's, whom we shall always be happy to render service to.

22. A TYPICAL ENVELOPE ADDRESSED TO JAMES KINNERSLEY

But several writers complain that he has not replied or agreed to an interview. One letter of January 1796, beginning 'Dear Friend', goes on:

What the D ... l is the matter with you? An old woman (Mrs Pierce) has almost fritted herself to death thro' your neglect, and I have been not a little plagued on account of it.

Another letter, of 30th March 1797, written from the Stock Exchange, complains about the writer's clients:

[They] informed me that they cannot get any answer from you respecting the conclusion of settling what must be pleasant to the interest of all parties concerned'.[100]

This may simply be the law's delays, but it suggests that James Kinnersley was too distracted by his other interests to spend enough time on financial and legal business. It is also possible that his health was already failing.

He died in November 1798 at the age of seventy six, and his memorial is in Eardisland church. His will shows that, like John Stead and the Sprotts, he had invested heavily in land. He left to his wife and her heirs and assigns, the manor of Whitton, several messuages, farms, lands, and tenements in Shropshire, including a messuage, farm and several coppice woods in the parish of Onibury, together with 'diverse messuages and lands' in the county of Cardigan. His widow, Lucy, lived on at the Broad Gate until 1813. During her widowhood, she bought a piece of land south of the town ditch from Samuel Yate Sprott, so doubling its width. In October 1806 she made a new application for the lease of the Wheatsheaf Inn which specifically mentions that the dungeon (in the space under the east tower) is not included. This suggests that at this time it was accessed through the cellar of the Wheatsheaf Inn or rather, that of its neighbour, Chandler's Cottage, and that the Corporation still had an interest in it.[101]

People with money to spare had, as we have seen, usually invested it in property. This often involved taking out loans. There were few banks, as we know them, in country areas, but commerce involved credit, and there had always existed a complicated system of loans across all classes, and in national and international trade. This was partly because the gold and silver from which coins were made were generally in short supply. That helped to avoid inflation, but it meant that credit was widely used to facilitate buying and selling.

Many loans were made among family members and friends and acquaintances, and debts were very often passed from one to another. John Stead, for example, seems to have been responsible for the debts of his brother-in-law, Valentine Dawes. We also see in the wills of Alice Dawes and her niece, Anne Stead, that loans were paid off, or remitted by the testator to family members or friends, or passed down to heirs. Anne Pryce, in her will of 1748, left to Thomas Yate 'the hundred pound bond that he is bound to me in on his Father's account'. Later, in Samuel Sprott's will, we read that

'There is due by mortgage from John Yate, father of Thomas Yate 250 and interest – he gave to Henry Yate, brother of Thomas Yate, 50 and the interest thereof part of the same, and other 200 and interest among the sisters of Thomas Yate equally'.

Trust and a code of honour were extremely important. The swearing of oaths and payment of small coins 'in earnest' often took the place of written contracts (the shaking of hands is still regarded as a seal on a commercial agreement). But, very soon, sealed bonds, drawn up by lawyers and witnessed, took the place of money, and could be exchanged as such. This, of course, brought more business to James Kinnersley. Bonds of this kind were again passed on to friends or relatives. In her will of February 14th 1741, Anne Stead left to her niece, Alice Mary Pulley, 'the money which my father, Mr John Stead, gave her a note of his hand for, as also the interest of it...[and] my aunt Mrs Alice Dawes's share of the money which can be Received or Recovered on the bond for Mr Cookes of Burchell, now in the possession of Mr Alin of Amiley'.

Mortgages also played a major part in the acquisition of property. Laws passed after the Restoration protected the borrowers from losing their land if they defaulted, by allowing them to extend the contract or to pay a rent. Charging interest was frowned upon if it took the form of usury, but since 1571 lenders had been permitted to charge interest to allow money to return to circulation. This enabled widows, for instance, to make a living from lending money. In 1690 the Bank of England was founded, and, increasingly, commercial banks were appearing, first in London and then in the provinces.

All of this fuelled the immense investment in land and property in the eighteenth century by people like the Steads, the Sprotts and the Kinnersleys. Since attorneys were so deeply involved as financial intermediaries, it is unsurprising that lawyers became bankers, particularly those known as 'money-scriveners' who acted partly as estate agents and partly as financial providers.[102] In the 1730s one member of the Sprott family, the attorney,

John Baldwin, lived as a widower with his two clerks at 17 Broad Street, the house of his aunt, Miss Isabella Sprott. He was a financial intermediary for many of his clients, borrowing, lending and investing for them as well as for himself.

James Kinnersley's second son by his first marriage, James Kinnersley the younger, was also a lawyer and a banker. He did not live at the Broad Gate - he was thirty when his father married again - but he owned or leased 23-23a Mill Street for a year in 1795. He operated as a banker in Ludlow, but lived at the Lynch in Eardisland. In 1799, soon after his father's death, he paid the Marquess of Bath £14,000 for various manorial lordships, including Eardisland. In Ludlow he joined the banking firm of Coleman, Davies and Kinnersley, founded by his father and in existence by 1787 or earlier. It was registered at Leominster as well as Ludlow and when it was later joined by Edward Wellings, a Ludlow mercer, it became Kinnersley, Coleman and Wellings. The *Ludlow Guide* of 1801 reports that 'for the accommodation of the Public and the benefit of Trade, there is a bank under the firm of Kinnersley, Wellings and Co. where business of every branch is punctually and honourably executed'. The bank may have operated at the Broad Gate itself or very near it, for in 1812 it was described by Felton as being at the lower end of Broad Street.

Banks had become essential as the building boom depended on credit, but they were still risky for lenders. On 15th February 1802, the *Hereford Journal* reported that:

During the night of Wednesday last, the Banking-office of Messrs. Kinnersley and Co. of Ludlow was broken into by some villains who were ignorant that the property is every evening removed to a place of greater security – by which, after an industrious search, they found themselves completely disappointed in their expectations.

In the 1820s there was also a series of bankruptcies. In 1824 Edward

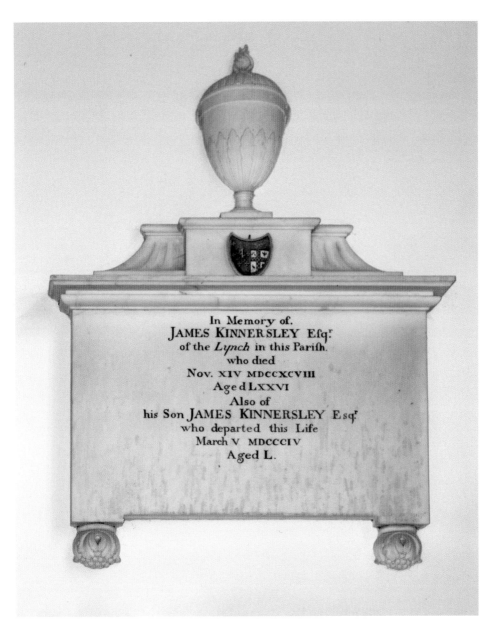

23. MEMORIAL TO JAMES KINNERSLEY AND HIS SON IN EARDISLAND CHURCH

Prodgers was bankrupted, and, long after James Kinnersley the younger's death, his partners Coleman and Wellings were declared bankrupt in 1824 and 1826.

In spite of not living at the house, James the younger was involved in a scheme that might have made a difference to the Broad Gate. In 1799 he was described as a proprietor of the Leominster Canal Navigation Company. He and his father were bankers for the company, and also joint proprietors of the Herefordshire and Gloucestershire Canal. Both Kinnersleys had already, in 1793, been involved in an abortive scheme to build a canal linking Liverpool with Bristol, part of which would have run round the edge of Ludlow, passing immediately below the Broad Gate, and linking with a branch at Leominster. This was a time of great enthusiasm for building rural canals to link with the canals running from industrial cities, to transport coal and manufactured goods more cheaply and easily than by road. The Ludlow section would have entered the town at Bromfield and run west round the Castle, between the town wall and the Teme, crossing Lower Broad Street in the town ditch below the Broad Gate. A petition was presented to Parliament in 1793 to allow shares in the scheme to be sold. It was signed by Lord Clive and other landowners and interested parties, among whom were the Rev. Samuel Sneade, Ellen Sneade's father, and both James Kinnersleys. The elder Kinnersley invested £1,000 (the second equal highest investment), and his son, the younger James, invested £500. Another interested party was Thomas Coleman, the Kinnersleys' banking partner. According to Felton's *A Description of the Town of Ludlow* (1812):

> *a navigable canal from Leominster to Stourport … after contending with immense difficulties, has been carried a few miles below Tenbury in Worcestershire, but from a failure of money, the pressure of the war, or want of enterprising spirit, the work has stood still for some years; however, it is probable that this desirable object will at some future*

*period be completed ... It was in contemplation to make a branch
canal from Wooferton to Ludlow; which probably will be done after
the completion of the original design.*

However, the plan, even in a truncated form, was clearly going to be
too expensive and it was abandoned. A map of the time showed the canal
from Bristol to Chester running east to west below the Broad Gate, wrongly
anticipating what was never to be. Had it been built it would have made the
Broad Gate look even more like a castle, with its own moat.

The Leominster Canal, however, was partly constructed. Eighteen and
a half miles ran between Leominster and Southnet Wharf, near Mamble,
where there were collieries, and this was the stretch which had been opened in
December 1796. The coal it carried sold at 15s per ton, half its previous price.
The canal was used for fifty years, but it was never financially successful, as
canals faced increasing competition from the railways. It was sold in 1858 to
the Shrewsbury and Hereford Railway Company. The shareholders received
only £16 for every hundred invested, so it turned out to have been a bad
investment for the Kinnersleys and their heirs.[103]

For all his enthusiasm for new methods of transport, James Kinnersley the
elder may have been responsible for defending the Broad Gate itself against
the forces of progress. On 12th September 1792, an alarming announcement
appeared in the *Hereford Journal*:

> *NOTICE IS HEREBY GIVEN*
>
> *that application is intended to be made in Parliament the next session
> for an Act for Paving, Widening, Repairing, Cleaning, Watching and
> Lighting the Streets, Lanes, Ways, Passages and Places within the
> Town of LUDLOW and the Precincts thereof, in the County of Salop;
> for removing of present and prevention of future, Encroachments,
> Nuisances and Annoyances therein; for taking down a certain Gate
> called Broad Gate, and certain Freehold and Leasehold Messuages*

or Tenements adjoining the said Gate or certain parts thereof, in the several possessions of James Kinnersley, John Sheward, James Mantle and Richard Careless; and a certain other Gate called Corve Gate … and also certain Leasehold Messuages or Tenements or parts thereof on the east side of Broad Street and the south side of King Street, for the purpose of widening the streets adjoining the said Messuages or Tenements, widening the Passages in some of the other Streets and stopping up a certain Lane or Way leading from the Broad Gate to the lower end of the Way or Lane called Merryvale; for regulating the drivers of Carts and other Carriages within the said Town and the Precincts thereof, and for other purposes.

The notice was no doubt inserted by Ludlow Corporation, which owned all the leasehold properties, including the Broad Gate. The 'other purposes' are not specified, but these ambitious alterations were to be paid for by enclosing Whitcliffe Common, Corve Meadow and another meadow from Old Midsummer's Day to Old Candlemas Day, and presumably charging for grazing there. Corve Gate disappeared at this time as a result of the scheme, but the rest of the buildings remain. Did James Kinnersley exert his considerable influence in the town to modify the plan or did Parliament refuse to countenance it? It was not the last time that the removal of the Broad Gate was to be suggested. The building did, however, have its admirers. Joseph Bullock, a weaver, who lived in Bell Lane, wrote, rather awkwardly, in *The Beauties of Ludlow: a Poem 1818*:

The handsome Broad Gate, which so firmly doth stand,
When passed up through is an entrance grand.[104]

James Kinnersley the younger was ambitious to make his mark. Like his father, he was well acquainted with all the leading lights in the area, including Richard Payne Knight of Downton Castle, who was another shareholder in the Leominster Canal Navigation Company, and in 1802 he was elected Vice-President of the Agricultural Society of Hereford, whose President was Thomas Andrew Knight of Elton, the renowned horticulturist. But in March 1804, the *Monthly Magazine* was reporting the death at the Lynch of a paralytic stroke, 'J. Kinnersley Esq, Clerk of the Peace for the county and one of the partners in the Ludlow and Leominster banking houses'. The Lynch was left to Elizabeth Kinnersley, his second cousin. Like the Sprotts, the Kinnersley descendants were involved in several court cases, and there were disputes over the disposition of the family's estates after Lucy Kinnersley's death. Although he died in 1799, the elder James Kinnersley's will was not proved until 1808, four years after the death of his son James. Despite bequeathing a large amount of land and property, he seems to have left debts, and his creditors included, or were represented by, his old colleague, Thomas Coleman of Leominster, who was bankrupt by 1824. Elizabeth Kinnersley, now Smythies, filed a bill limiting the funds claimed by the creditors to £12,000, but this was contested by Coleman.

The case was first heard in Chancery in 1815 and dragged on, like Jarndyce v. Jarndyce, for another seventeen years. Finally, in 1832, Lord Brougham, who could no longer remember whether it was Coleman v. Smythies or Smythies v. Coleman, ruled that 'all the landed estates embraced by certain trust deeds, and not a limited part only, should be devoted to the payment of the deceased's remaining debts'. As the *Hereford Journal* for 22nd August commented:

> *The subject matter of this cause has been the object of litigation since the year 1815, and during the progress of the suit, it in various forms came under the consideration of no less than five successive Chancery Judges.*

According to the Easter Book for 1813, the widow, Lucy Kinnersley, was still living at the Broad Gate, but she died soon after, and in August that year the *Salopian Journal* advertised a forthcoming sale at the Angel in Ludlow, in four lots. Lot 1 was 'a capital and spacious dwelling-house called the Broad Gate, suitable for the accommodation of a genteel family, most desirably situate in the Broad-street, Ludlow, late the residence of Mrs Kinnersley'. The sales particulars detail exactly the extent of the house and grounds at that time:

> ... *on the First Floor, Six large Bed rooms and a Laundry, with attics above; on the Ground Floor, a handsome Entrance Hall, Drawing Room, Breakfast and Dining Parlours, Kitchen, Pantries, with excellent Offices thereunder; Cellars and Stabling; a Hot-house, with a large Garden, inclosed with a lofty brick wall, facing the south, stocked well with choice Fruit Trees, and commanding a most delightful view of Whitcliffe Hill and the River Teme.*

The lot also included two gardens below the town wall and the cottage in Merry Vale (Silk Mill Lane) 'adjoining the stable and fronting Merry Vale, now occupied by Samuel Powell, plumber and glazier', which James Kinnersley the elder had bought. Lot 2 refers to a dwelling in Lower Broad Street with garden and yard; this is almost certainly the cottage on the front of the western tower which would around 1825 be demolished to make way for the legal chambers. Lot 3 was a house at the bottom of Mill Street in the town ditch, and Lot 4 five houses in the Vineyard with a separate garden. The particulars were to be obtained from Lucy Kinnersley's nephew, the Rev. George Dansey Pardoe, or from Messrs. Henry and William Lloyd, solicitors, the first indication we have of the Lloyds' interest in the property.

The house, or more precisely the lease on the house, as the freehold still belonged to Ludlow Corporation, was unsold, for want of buyers, presumably because times were hard towards the end of the Napoleonic Wars. So in October 1813 the lease passed to Lucy Kinnersley's nephew and executor, George Dansey Pardoe, still for an annual rent of 32s. By the following year this lease had been acquired by the Lloyd family. In November 1814, George Dansey Pardoe petitioned the Corporation to hand the lease over to Henry Lloyd, a local attorney, and it was sold to him for £1,720.[105] In 1816, the Easter book shows that Henry and a sister and four maids had come to live there. His wife, Thomasin, had died aged forty-eight in 1814, after nine years of childbearing between 1795 and 1804. The eight children, being mostly under the age of sixteen, were not included among the occupants. Henry Lloyd had practised in Ludlow with his brother, William, from about 1797. They were well-known to the Sprotts and probably to the Kinnersleys as well, as their names appear in the many legal documents, wills and lawsuits involving the families, and they may already have known the house well.

24. *A WATERCOLOUR SKETCH OF THE BROAD GATE FROM LOWER BROAD STREET,
painted in 1814, by George Jones R.A., showing the house attached to the west tower which
would soon be demolished to make way for the legal chambers. At least three horses are needed
to drag the cart up the steep incline under the arch, prior to Telford's improvements*

– 6 –

THE EIGHTEENTH-CENTURY HOUSE AND ITS CONTENTS

When Henry Lloyd took over the lease of the Broad Gate in 1814, the house would have been much as the Sprotts had left it after their major renovations in the mid-eighteenth century, though some of the domestic improvements in the kitchen and brewery may have been installed in the interval between his signing the lease and occupying the house in 1816. The Sprotts and the Kinnersleys had both consolidated the estate by buying up parcels of land and properties in Silk Mill Lane and in the town ditch, as well as in Lower Broad Street, so that the house sat in a considerable amount of land above and below the town wall. On the outside, the drum towers and the north-facing front were battlemented. The surface was now rendered and cut to look like stone, as the towers remain today, suggesting a fortified building. The cellars on each side of the arch, accessed at ground level from the road and the pathway, were no longer needed for the collection of tolls or as a prison. The door to the prison under the eastern tower, last used during the Civil War, was reached through the cellar of Chandler's Cottage below the tower and was now part of that leasehold. The cellar under the dining-room was a lower extension of the kitchen, while the cellars under the western tower had several different uses. The central staircase, built into the medieval back wall of the drum towers, led from the

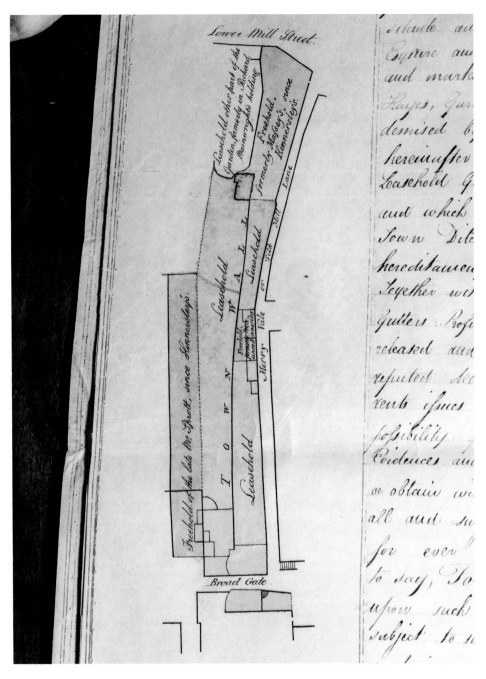

25. A MAP OF THE BROAD GATE ESTATE IN 1815
showing the leasehold and freehold property. This part of Maryvale is now Silk Mill Lane

west cellar to the attic, with access to each floor. These stairs were now the servants' back stairs.

The 'ground' floor was reached by the semicircular flight of steps to the front door which brought one to the level of the top of the town wall, rather than that of the street far below. It consisted of a large entrance hall, three parlours, one of them panelled, and a kitchen and scullery in the east tower. Corresponding to the kitchen, there was also a room in the west tower which may have been a service room of some kind. It could have been entered from the scullery, between the towers. In the hall, pride of place was now given to the imposing oak staircase. Dating from the Sprotts' time, it had probably been brought in by Pritchard from elsewhere and did not quite fit. It led to the first floor where there were six bedrooms and a dressing-room for the west bedroom.

A dressing-room or closet was a private space very often used as an office and this one contained a built-in writing desk. A closet could be anything from a highly decorated room to a large cupboard. Samuel Pepys had a 'closet', but his wife had a 'study'. Its main purpose was its use as a private area, away from family and servants, perhaps originally for prayer and meditation, but later in grand houses a private sanctum at the end of a long *enfilade* of rooms where only those nearest to the owner could be received. It was often an area where private collections of books, papers, *objets d'art* or cabinets of curiosities were kept. At Strawberry Hill in one of his several closets, Horace Walpole kept a collection of drawings in 'a sanctuary, not to be shown to all the profane that come to see the house'.[106] In smaller houses it could be simply a curtained-off area, but it was generally a small room with its own windows and a lockable door. It would have had its own fireplace, which, given the difficulties of heating large rooms, would have made it a welcome space for reading, working or receiving intimate friends in the winter.

In the Broad Gate, the small room with two doors, one on to the landing and another into the west bedroom, was probably intended as a dressing room. It had a built-in wardrobe and room for a bed, but, as it contained a built-in writing desk, it must also have been a place for working. The room's two functions were interchangeable; and it might have been used by either the master or the mistress of the house. In the 1718 will and inventory of Francis Herbert of Oakly Park,[107] the room containing a 'hanging press' (wardrobe) as well as a desk is described as 'the Master's dressing room', though in Herbert's house, Lymore Park, near Montgomery, he had a 'working closet'. In many Broad Street houses there is a small room to the right or left of the front door, where business could be conducted without having to receive visitors in the private part of the house. It could also be conveniently turned into a shop. In the Broad Gate the layout is different. John Stead's house had a 'study' and a closet, but that was before the fire, so it is impossible to know exactly where it was. The doctors, lawyers and bankers who lived there later may have used one of the parlours off the hall to receive clients. The upstairs closet is more likely to have been a private space belonging to the mistress of the house.

For women in a busy household with a demanding husband, children and servants, a private closet was often the only room they could call their own, and where their privacy was meant to be inviolate. Ophelia is shocked when Hamlet appears to her in her closet, and Clarissa Harlowe in Richardson's novel (1748) uses her closet as her only safe retreat when beset by her relatives. These fictional examples are borne out by Mrs Delaney, the flower painter, who, as a young girl in 1715 or 16, was grateful for her own closet to retire to when being forced by her uncle into an unwanted marriage:

I took great delight in a closet I had which was furnished with little drawings and cut paper of my own doing. I had a desk and shelves for my books.[108]

Although closets were very small, they were often highly decorated.

Sometimes they were elaborately arranged print rooms. Mrs Lybbe Powys exclaims with delight at a dressing room at Fawley Court in Buckinghamshire:

> *the dressing-room … is prettier than 'tis possible to imagine, the most curious India paper as birds, flowers &c. put up as different pictures in frames of the same, with festoons, India baskets, figures, &c. on a peagreen paper.* [109]

Even those on the ground floor used for business could be very impressive. A room to the right of the front door at 18 Broad Street is furnished with fine earlier panelling, no doubt brought in for the bank manager to impress his clients. At the White House at Suckley, near Worcester, the first-floor dressing-room, only accessible through the best bedroom, is a 'richly decorated marquetry closet, its panelling with contrasting veneers'.[110] It has no desk, but another small room downstairs has a built-in desk designed, again, by Pritchard. One of the most impressive dressing-rooms is the oval room designed by John Nash at Llanerchaerron in Ceredigion. At Attingham, near Shrewsbury, there are two small rooms, one octagonal, the other circular, at opposite ends of the house, one for the master and one for the mistress of the house, appropriately decorated. In 1750, there was 'a dressing room, fitted up Gothick' at Arbury Hall. The closet or dressing-room at the Broad Gate is much less pretentious, but it has a cornice round the walls, a strong key pattern decoration on the central beam, and a broken pediment over the writing desk. By the nineteenth century the room was probably used more as a dressing room, but the desk was available, together with a peephole in the shutters so that whoever was working at it could see what was happening in Broad Street even when they were closed.

In two of the bedrooms on this floor there were rococo chimney-pieces of a kind which was almost certainly once present in the ground-floor parlours as well. Two of these parlours had elaborate cornices. The cornice in the west parlour at the oldest end of the house was in an earlier baroque style, that in the room next to it had a later, more restrained neo-classical design of wheat ears, a typical Adamesque decoration. Tastes became simpler as the eighteenth century continued. The ceiling in the hall itself was not highly decorated, as in John Stead's original house, but retained part of the simpler cornice from his rebuilding.

In the past, the 'great' chamber or best bedroom would have been the grandest room in a house, but the best room by this time was the drawing-room, which in Georgian town houses was usually on the first floor or piano nobile, so that it could stretch the whole width of the house. It is possible that the bedroom at the east end of

26. THE DRESSING-ROOM WRITING DESK
with broken pediment

the Broad Gate, with its fine chimney-piece and long windows, was at first intended as an upstairs front drawing-room, or 'forestreet' room, looking onto the street, but here the largest of the ground floor parlours became the drawing-room, and the first floor room was, perhaps, the best guest bedroom. Below this room, the newly-built parlour to the left of the front door, was panelled and is most likely to have been the now fashionable dining-parlour, although the 1813 sales notice says that there was also a 'breakfast-parlour'.

In the time of John Stead, a parlour might have been used for any purpose, eating, sleeping, working, childcare, as well as receiving visitors, but the rooms gradually took on more specialized functions. Beds, which had earlier been seen as objects of status, were now removed to 'chambers' or bedrooms. By the mid-eighteenth century, 'Mr Good's house' near Bromyard, designed by Pritchard, had a 'best parlour' and a 'common parlour'. So in the 1813 sales particulars for the Broad Gate, one of the parlours is designated 'drawing-room' and the others as 'dining-parlour' and 'breakfast-parlour'. Before the mid-eighteenth century food could have been eaten in any parlour, but with the growth of social entertaining, a room was set aside for this purpose, and was often panelled, because panelling was thought not to retain food odours as damask or tapestry might have done.[111] The Broad Gate's dining-room was provided with a large china cupboard, as well as a set of corner shelves for display. One mystery in the house is a large walk-in cupboard space off the passage leading to the garden door. It may once have been entered from the adjoining parlour, but seems to have been cut off by the replacement of the staircase. It would be an ordinary storage space, were it not that it retains a cornice and may have been intended as a display area for the parlour behind it.

When the Broad Gate was put on the market in the 1940s, the sales particulars revealed that there was still a great deal of Georgian furniture in the house. We do not know exactly how the parlours were furnished in the eighteenth century, though we do know that in the first half of the century it was usual for furniture to be arranged formally around the edges of the room. Parlours at the time were generally square and quite small, but looking-glasses were used to suggest more space as well as to reflect candle-light in the evening. This was particularly striking in the dining parlour, where reflections from glass and silver and polished mahogany would have been multiplied. There was no clutter, objects were arranged carefully (even dishes set out as a course or buffet on a polished mahogany table were strictly symmetrical), and the emphasis was on order and elegance. By the end of the century, however, things were becoming much less formal. In Jane Austen's *Persuasion (1818)*, in the 'unmodernized' Great House of the Musgroves, a gentry family:

> *They went to sit the whole half hour in the old-fashioned square parlour, with a small carpet and shining floor, to which the present daughters of the house were gradually giving the proper air of confusion by a grand piano forte and a harp, flower-stands and little tables placed in every direction. Oh! could the originals of the portraits against the wainscot, could the gentlemen in brown velvet and the ladies in blue satin have seen what was going on, have been conscious of such an overthrow of all order and neatness! The portraits themselves seemed to be staring in astonishment.*

Inventories for other houses in the latter half of the eighteenth century suggest that there was a huge increase in the acquisition of fine mahogany furniture, upholstered chairs, floor carpets, chintz and ceramics, which were all newly fashionable items, emphasising pleasure and comfort, and replacing the wall-hangings, heavy oak furniture and pewter of the seventeenth century. In the family wills, however, it is clear that certain objects associated with the family history were still highly valued and passed down through the generations. In 1715, Anne Sprott, née Lockier, Samuel and Henry's grandmother, left to Henry her silver basin and ewer, 'the same always to remain in the Sprott family'. Her daughter, Anne Pryce, was to receive 'one of my great gold rings, either that which was my mother's or that which was my aunt Fewtrell's'. Anne Pryce herself left to her nephew Samuel 'the great salt' which she had lent to his mother, some 'fine old coin' and some family papers. Her sister, Isabella, in 1732 bequeathed to her nephew, Thomas, 'my grandfather's signet ring', no doubt another Lockier heirloom; and Samuel Sprott in his will of 1753 left his nephew and heir, Thomas Yate, his watch and seals. Two hundred years later, Ethel Mary Lloyd in her will, gave her niece, Mary Louisa Lloyd, 'my gold ring set with pearls and inset with my great-grandmother's hair'. These objects, which came by descent rather than acquisition 'created a visual narrative of the family history'.[112]

Portraits were of particular importance. In an age before photography they might have been valued for sentimental reasons as the only visual record of loved ones, but they served another purpose as well, namely, to commemorate the subject. Alice Dawes, John Stead's sister-in-law, lived frugally, but she possessed several family portraits. She left the picture of her husband,

27. A MINIATURE OF THOMASIN
Henry Lloyd's first wife, with the ring which was passed down to her great-grand-daughter, Mary

Valentine Dawes, to her nephew, Valentine Stead, probably his godson, and her own to her niece, Anne Stead, 'immediately after the death of my sister Stead their mother, who is to have the use of both the said pictures during her natural life'. Anne Stead, in turn, left 'my aunt, Mrs Alice Dawes picture' to her cousin, Alice Mary Pulley. Anne Pryce left her nephew, Samuel Sprott, 'the picture of myself to be hanged near his own', and Samuel made sure in his will that 'his pictures are to go with his principal inheritance for the benefit of his heir, only his wife is to use them for her life'. In stipulating that they were to pass down the family, older members ensured that there would be a continual reminder of their presence. Anne Pryce insisted that she should be clearly visible in a prominent position, exerting her authority from beyond the grave, together with the reminder of the Agard ancestry that was so important to her. There is no specific mention of a portrait of Samuel's wife, Mary, so perhaps the Agard connection trumped that of the Childes.

In his great book, *Distinction: a Social Critique of the Judgement of Taste*, the French sociologist Pierre Bourdieu (1930-2002) writes:

> *Every material inheritance is, strictly speaking, also a cultural inheritance. Family heirlooms not only bear material witness to the age and continuity of the lineage and so consecrate its social identity; they also contribute in a practical way to its spiritual reproduction, that is, to transmitting the values, virtues and competences which are the basis of legitimate membership in bourgeois dynasties.* [113]

This was still true in the nineteenth century, when Henry Lloyd had portraits painted of himself and his first wife, Thomasin (see Fig. 39).

Some of the family wills of the Steads and the Sprotts in the eighteenth century reveal what other kinds of objects were possessed and which of them were most valued. Alice Dawes, Priscilla Stead's sister, was the widow of Valentine Dawes. He and his father had at one time owned 49 Broad Street (now Oriel House) and the Jester public house next to it. They had spent a great deal of money on them and other ventures, and John Stead later had to rescue his brother-in-law from debt. [114]

After her husband's death, Alice, like many widows, lived in lodgings, possibly in a single room, and could keep only what was necessary or particularly precious to her. The possessions left to relatives in her will of 1722 are all her worldly goods: the furniture in her room, pictures, looking glasses, dishes, her clothes and a large quantity of linen. She owned a bed with a bolster and two blankets, one inlaid table and one small table, two looking glasses, one with an embroidered frame, possibly stump-work done in her younger days, two easy chairs, one made of 'blue Kidderminster stuff', a fire shovel and tongs, twelve pewter plates, four earthenware plates, two 'mazarines' [metal dishes], a 'Brasil [hardwood] stand dish' [for pens], an inlaid dressing box, four portraits, one pair of holland sheets, two pairs of flaxen sheets, five pairs of hempen sheets, one dozen damask napkins, one dozen flaxen napkins, one dozen hempen napkins, a dozen and a half of diaper napkins and six huckaback napkins, and a quantity of wearing apparel. Her estate as a whole was valued at £17.10s, which would be several thousand pounds today, so she had clearly salvaged something from the wreck of her husband's fortune. The frequent references to linen in these wills reflect the importance of sheets, cloths and napkins in the eighteenth century household, where napkins were used at every meal, and hands and faces wiped with warm, damp cloths after eating. An inventory of linen was taken every year.[115] Damask and flaxen were finer linen than huckaback or hempen in an age when both linen and clothing were defined by the material from which they were manufactured.

When she made her will eight years later, Isabella Sprott, a spinster but well provided for, possessed the latest silver items for the new practice of tea and coffee-making. Among the bequests in her will of 1730 are a silver tea-kettle, a silver sugar dish, a silver coffee pot, a silver teapot and slop basin, a large silver salver and spoons, and a silver tea canister. All of these were left to female relatives. At this time the practice of drinking hot, non-alcoholic drinks was becoming increasingly important in the lives of well-to-do women. Tea, like coffee and chocolate, was drunk at breakfast and after dinner. Men met their friends and acquaintances at taverns or coffee-houses, or in card and oyster clubs at the principal inns, but for women it was a chance to socialise at home in a ritual which was under their control. At first, tea was extremely expensive and so were the silver items connected with its preparation and consumption. A series of poor harvests in the 1780s, however, meant that ale was scarce, and, since water was unsafe, tea and other drinks made with boiling water became a necessity for all classes. The price of tea came down quite quickly and the tax on its import was very much reduced by Pitt the Younger in 1784, but there was still a tax on silver, which was in any case beyond the reach of most people. As the middle classes, as well as those lower down the social scale, took up tea-drinking there was a demand for non-porous ceramic teapots which could withstand boiling water, and for bowls, saucers and jugs to go with them. Ceramics copied and replaced silver for almost all tableware, including knife and fork handles. At the same time, factories on the continent such as Dresden, Meissen and Sèvres were discovering how to make a hard-paste porcelain which could match the qualities of the Chinese porcelain flooding into the European market. Some of these products were exquisite and intended for display. If they were in use, they were jealously guarded by the mistress of the house, who presided over the tea table, kept the keys to the tea caddy and even washed the china herself.

Continental porcelain was imported in quantities, but cheaper versions were soon being made in Britain. A soft-paste porcelain, such as that made at Bow or Chelsea in the 1750s, was rapidly superseded by the more reliable soapstone or bone ash of factories like Worcester or Derby and the creamware of Josiah Wedgwood, who saw the possibilities in a new mass market. After the 1780s, Staffordshire factories like New Hall, who were now making a form of hard-paste porcelain, gave over most of their production to the tea and coffee services which were so much in demand. In Jane Austen's *Northanger Abbey* (1818), General Tilney tries to impress Catherine with his new breakfast set:

> *He was enchanted by her approbation of his taste, confessed it to be neat and simple, thought it right to encourage the manufacture of his country; and for his part, to his uncritical palate, the tea was as well flavoured from the clay of Staffordshire, as from that of Dresden or Sêve [Sèvres].*

Staffordshire, of course, and Coalbrookdale were comparatively near to Ludlow, and were centres for innovation in the production of china, so local

28. A NEW HALL TEA AND COFFEE SERVICE
made around 1790, and as elegant as any continental porcelain

households would have been well aware of what was on offer. For the middle classes and above, ceramics had, by the end of the eighteenth century, replaced pewter and silver at family meals as well as in company. Parson Woodforde thought it worth recording in his diary in June 1794, when he was dining with Mr Mellish, that 'we had a very good dinner, all on China and everything very tasty'.[116]

Silver objects, however, were still prized and displayed. In the will of Joyce Sprott the younger of 1797, we find a silver porringer, sugar dish, spoons, tongs and an infinite number of silver salt cellars, but it also included a set of 'pencil' (painted or decorated) china, two and a half dozen china plates, two pairs of china mugs and two half-pint china mugs. Some of these were left to the men in the family. Joyce also had plenty of linen to leave her female relatives, though now the sheets and table-cloths were simply described as 'fine'.

All these precious objects were carefully tended by the successive

29. INDIVIDUAL OVENS BUILT INTO THE KITCHEN WALLS
with fireboxes below. The oven next to the window, was for keeping dishes warm, proving
bread or drying out, with, to its right, the pastry oven for bread, cake or confectionery

mistresses of the house, who, as time went on, spent less and less time in the kitchen, which in most town houses was in the basement. At the Broad Gate it was on the 'ground' floor, though high above the street, in a room in the eastern drum tower which had been in use since the thirteenth century. It faced south-east and led to a scullery, larder and store cupboard in the area over the arch, from which there was a very good view of everything that went on in Lower Broad Street. If there had once been a medieval open fire and spit in the large fireplace, it would by this time have been replaced by a more up-to-date iron range and numerous ovens, what Jane Austen calls 'stoves and hot closets'. The equipment for food preparation was becoming increasingly specialised. At one time cooking might have taken place on any wood fire in any room with a chimney, but the change from wood to coal as a fuel meant the arrival as permanent fixtures of purpose-built iron ranges, trivets and pulleys for turning roasts. The large range, set into the fireplace, would have had a fire-grate in the centre, and a masonry hob at each end. Large pots and kettles would be hung over the fire, and pans set to boil and simmer on the bars in front. But the main function of this fire would be roasting. For the middle classes, meat would have been cheap and plentiful and was eaten at almost every meal, supplemented by fish and game from the countryside around. Some was boiled or baked, but large joints were roasted. They would be mounted on iron spits which would be rotated in front of the glowing coals in the grate. By this time, the turning of the spits would be done by a mechanical device known as a 'spit-jack', which, on the right of the fireplace, rotated loops of chain which turned a pulley at the end of the spit.

As well as the central range in the kitchen at the Broad Gate, there were also two other large ovens built into the thick medieval walls, each with its own fire-box and ash-pit, so that food could be cooked or kept warm at different temperatures. The custom at this period was for food at formal meals to be set out as buffets or courses of five or more dishes, though when Parson Woodforde dined with the Bishop of Norwich, there were two courses of twenty dishes.[117] At each course, elegantly and symmetrically arranged on the table, there would be both savoury and sweet dishes, hot and cold. When people had eaten enough of the first course, it would be removed and replaced with a similar choice, though with more emphasis on sweet dishes. Normally, there would be two courses, especially if guests were expected. Mrs Bennet in *Pride and Prejudice,* 1813, inviting Bingley and Darcy to dinner, 'did not think any thing less than two courses could be good enough for a man on whom she had such anxious designs, or satisfy the appetite and pride of one who had ten thousand a year'. The main courses would be followed by a dessert of fruit, nuts and sometimes, confectionery. When

30. THE WORKING KITCHEN AS IT MAY HAVE LOOKED IN 1814
The metal plate on the window-sill, now boarded over, was used for heating sauces and keeping food warm. It had its own firebox

Parson Woodforde dined at home with his niece, Nancy, who lived with him, they had what he calls a 'family dinner', one course of soup or fish with a choice of at least two roasts, and 'garden stuff'. But when he had guests or dined away from home, a typical menu for eight people might be:

First Course: half a dozen fine mackerel boiled, a saddle of mutton roasted, boiled tongue and spinach, half a dozen pigeons in a pie, hot currant and plain puddings.

Second Course: three spring chickens roasted, asparagus, berries, gooseberry tarts and tartlets.

Followed by a dessert of almonds, raisins, oranges and olives.

So much choice meant that dishes often had to be made in advance, and served in sauces, piping hot. In the Broad Gate kitchen, a metal plate set over the sill of the eastern window, much enlarged and set into a wall thirty-eight inches thick, could hold many saucepans and bains-maries to keep sauces hot. Again, it had its own fire-box below. Of the two extra ovens, the one nearer the window would have been used for keeping dishes warm, proving bread and drying ingredients; the other was a pastry oven for bread, cakes and confectionery.

Under the kitchen floor, in the drum-tower, there may once have been a well, accessed by a trap door through the flags, but around this time, the opening was covered and part of the lower tower converted into a large ice-house, a deep brick shaft with a domed roof. Normally, ice houses were constructed in the grounds of a house, near a river or lake. This one was unusual in being built in the house itself. Blocks of ice would have been brought up from the river in winter, broken into smaller pieces, stacked and rammed tight in the shaft and insulated with straw or hay bales behind a series of doors similarly insulated. The ice house was reached from the flight of curving stone steps leading from the kitchen to the north cellar, which is under the dining room floor, steps which are almost certainly the remains of the original medieval steps giving access to the upper floor of the east tower. In the north cellar itself there was also a vast meat safe or 'wet larder'. Here meat, whether slaughtered on the premises or not, was butchered into smaller joints and salted, potted or pickled so as to preserve it. No part of the animal was wasted. There were grooves in the floor to drain away excess blood or water, and an old stone chest for salt. The ice-house was conveniently close. Throughout the cellars were hooks for hanging hams and other joints. So Henry Lloyd had installed the latest domestic arrangements for himself, his sister, his eight children and four servants, and the cook had

31. THE BREW-HOUSE IN THE GROUND-LEVEL CELLAR IN THE WEST TOWER
In the nineteenth century the Broad Gate brewed beer on a large scale and sold off its surplus

ample provision for preparing, preserving and storing food, and for keeping it hot or cold.

On the west side of the arch, the cellars contained the passage way to the sally-port, which ran parallel to the arch, a wine cellar with good brick bins, and a room linking the two for the collector of tolls, with its own fireplace. The southern cellar, under the western tower and opening into the backyard, was a brewery or 'brewhouse' in the deeds, with two large copper-lined vats and an enormous tap, very similar to those in the service yard at Llanerchaeron, the Nash house near Aberaeron. The upper vat heated water which was then run off into a 'mash-tun' where it was mixed with malted barley and left to soak, then poured into the lower vat for boiling with hops. It was then cooled, poured into another tub with yeast and left to ferment, allowing the sugars to turn into alcohol. The Broad Gate is said to have brewed beer on quite a scale, and, like many households at the time, sold off its surplus, particularly after the 1830 Beerhouse Act, which enabled anyone to brew and sell beer on their own premises. The back yard, which was walled off from the town ditch, would have contained another well and probably pig-sties, and somewhere to dry washing. Workshops are mentioned in one of the leases.

There might also have been outdoor privies in this area. It is impossible to say whether the house had an internal earth closet, or when the first water closet appeared, but it would have discharged into the drains in the back yard from the south west corner of the house. The lavatory in the top floor of the Gatehouse, now incorporated into the present bathroom, is probably where the original water closet was placed, with its rather odd triangular window in the angle of the roof. Before this, the maids would have had to empty their slop pails with their contents from the chamber pots into the privies in the yard. In the particulars for the sale in 1940 two commodes are mentioned, but they are probably not that kind of 'convenience', since one is described as 'Chippendale'.

Before the eighteenth century, the town ditch had been used for various activities such as horticulture and building. Cottages had been put up against the wall itself, and a new square rampart had been constructed. At the far end, an industrial area was created in the wall itself, with its own flue. (This space was later used by Ludlow Grammar School as a store for

32. THE KITCHEN GARDEN, LOOKING WEST
The parapet of the town wall is to the left, with the inner wall at right behind the apple trees

dangerous chemicals.) The land, which was also leased with the Broad Gate, now provided ground for orchards and, perhaps, poultry.

On the top of the wall itself, and reached from the original medieval ground floor passage with its coved ceiling, was the 'upper' or pleasure garden next to the house, with flowers, shrubs and a long, narrow lawn. The 1885 map of Ludlow shows a summerhouse in a corner by the stables looking out over the river, but this has disappeared. The stables, opening into Silk Mill Lane, had room for two horses and a carriage. The manure from the horses would have been used in the garden, and an underground spring and pump nearby provided water for both horses and garden. Beyond the stables and coachman/gardener's cottage (acquired in the 1780s by James Kinnersley) lay the south-facing kitchen garden, with its warm bricks lining the stone street wall (which was possibly once an inner defensive wall). Here there were also extensive glass-houses for growing exotic fruit, and more

33. THE STABLE BUILDING VIEWED FROM SILK MILL LANE

fruit trees. The garden extended the whole length of Silk Mill Lane, about four hundred and fifty feet, and ran along the top of the town wall, with a drop on the southern side of over twenty feet to the town ditch below, and an uninterrupted view of Whitcliffe and the river Teme.

The extraordinary thing is that almost all of these features of the house and much of the garden remain today. Among the most charming survivals from the eighteenth century in the house itself is a naïve panel painting in the west bedroom showing Dinham Bridge and the Castle, probably painted in the 1730s. Although the various buildings in the far background have not been identified, the foreground details seem accurate enough, and show the new bridge of brick and stone which replaced the old wooden bridge in 1733. The picturesque ruin on the left may have been a later fanciful addition as it stands on what was the site of a quarry.

121

34. A PANEL PAINTING IN A BEDROOM AT THE BROAD GATE (1733 – 1740)
probably painted by an itinerant artist, showing Dinham Bridge and the Castle

Another intriguing feature is the name and date scratched on one of the panes in the kitchen window:

Thomas Morris April 9th 1792

Thomas Morris might have been a friend of the Kinnersleys or, more likely, a servant or craftsman. Around the same time, in Thomas Carlyle's house in Cheyne Row in Chelsea, a servant, John Tarbit Knowles, scratched the date, '7th March 1794', on a back window pane with the words 'cleaned all the windows and painted part in the 18 years of his age'.[118]

There is another example in Ludlow itself of a *graffito* scratched on a window:

William Lloyd 1817

This is at the Reader's House in a room on the first floor, so it is less likely to be the work of a servant, though it might have been scratched by

35. A LEADED LIGHT IN THE KITCHEN
with 'Thomas Morris April 9th 1792'
scratched on the glass

a child. It is also possible that, at the Broad Gate, Thomas Morris was the maker of the window itself, which is cut deep into the eastern wall of the drum tower and consists of leaded lights with some coloured panes. Craftsmen were often asked to sign their work if it was particularly well done.

An interesting innovation in the house is the early use of iron for the glazing bars in the north-facing windows of the hall and drawing room. The nearness of Coalbrookdale may account for this and for the presence of so many early cast-iron grates in the house. Another feature, fairly typical of Ludlow, is the reuse of older material. The kitchen door seems unlikely to have started life as a door; with its overall design of raised lozenges it looks more like the top of a chest. Some of the cupboard doors in the kitchen have clearly been recycled from earlier pieces of panelling. In spite of the many new and tempting luxury items, there was great emphasis on frugality and economy. The old ideas of production and self-sufficiency still prevailed and nothing was wasted.

The whole property of the Broad Gate, with its gardens, orchards, glasshouses, stables, pig-sties, brewery, ice-house and elegant reception rooms could be seen as a miniature, self-sufficient country estate, perched on the edge of the town. In 1814 it had every convenience needed to sustain the life of a prosperous, professional and 'genteel' family.

36. THE ARCH FROM THE SOUTH TODAY

— 7 —

THE LLOYDS
1814-1946

Ludlow was a magnet to the world around. While the Steads came from the north, the Sprotts from the east and the Kinnersleys from the south, the Lloyds came to Ludlow originally from the west – from Radnorshire. They were a landed family with farms and other property in the Builth area. Their pedigree can be traced back with certainty to Evan Lloyd of Cwmemliw, Disserth, who died in 1737, though, like many Welsh families, they claimed to be descended from Welsh princes, including Elystan Glodrydd, 'a powerful chieftain' who owned most of the land between the Severn and the Wye, and who died early in the eleventh century. The line allegedly descended through his son, Cadwgan, Lord of Builth and Brecon, down twelve generations to Thomas Lloyd ap Meredith the first, who took the surname Lloyd. He supported Henry VII at the Battle of Bosworth and became Lieutenant of the County of Brecon. From Rees Lloyd, his eldest son, came the Lloyds of Aberanell, who were the forebears of Evan Lloyd of Cwmemliw.

Evan Lloyd was probably born in about 1670. He appears to have been the only son in a family of eight children. In her will of 1772, one of his unmarried sisters, Mary Lloyd, mentions many nephews and nieces. She was, herself, quite well-to-do, since, when she died, she left £81 in respect of

125

37. CARVING OF THE NAME 'EVAN LL[OYD] 1722'
on a pew door in Disserth church

'money att interest'. In his own will, Evan describes himself as 'of Cwmemly'. Cwmemliw is a farm in the Carneddan Hills, near Disserth, about three miles north-north-east of Builth Wells. Sadly, the house burned down in the twentieth century, but in Disserth church one of the box pews has 'ELL 1722', carved on its door, and an Evan Lloyd was one of the churchwardens in 1730. His grandson, Evan Lloyd of Weobley, still owned the farm and the church pew in 1775. In his will of 1737, after bequests to his grandchildren, Jane and Evan, Evan Lloyd of Cwmemliw named his daughter-in-law, Mary, as his executrix, presumably because his eldest son, also Evan, born in 1699, had predeceased him.

On 13th May 1730 this son had married at Llanfihangel Abergwesyn, Breconshire, Mary Thomas (1773-1778), daughter of Edward Thomas of

126

Llwynmadoc, a few miles from Builth Wells. He died intestate on September 13th 1736 and administration was granted to his 'Relick', Mary. The inventory of his 'goods, chattels and cattle' amounted to £40.10s. Their three children, Gwen (born and died 1731), Jane (1732-1803), who married Thomas Davies of Disserth, and Evan (1734-1809), were all baptised at Disserth church.

This last Evan grew up in Disserth and married on 20th September 1760 Mary Harper of Llanelwedd, Radnorshire. In the ensuing fourteen years before her death in 1774, aged thirty-six, they had twelve children, including three sets of twins. The eldest were baptised at Disserth, but all the others at Weobley, where they moved in 1762. Evan's father had made a good marriage in allying himself with the Thomas family. His brother-in-law, Alban Thomas of Llwynmadoc, was agent to Lord Weymouth, Marquess of Bath, who owned land in the Weobley area, and from 1768 to 1809 Evan himself was Bailiff for the Marquess's estates in Weobley; this may account for his moving his family there and acquiring land in this district. He sold Cwmemliw to the Thomas family in about 1787 and another farm, Cefyndyrys in Llanelwedd, perhaps his wife's home, where his cousin by marriage, David Thomas, built a house. In Weobley he and his family lived in a large prominent house, known as 'the Bear', in the centre of the village. It had in the past been an inn, but in the eighteenth century it became a dwelling-house, no doubt for the Marquess's bailiff, where he could collect rents and run the borough for the Marquess's benefit. Weobley was a prime example of a pocket borough, with about forty houses giving their occupiers the right to vote, 'Mr Lloyd keeping open house for three days, and making entertainment the night before the election'.[119] At the Bear, an old drawing found under the floorboards of the house shows an unusual door in the centre of the first floor front which gave onto the porch of the front door below. From here the result of the election was announced.[120]

Evan Lloyd used his position in the borough to buy other leasehold and freehold property in Weobley, including the Bear Croft, which gave him the right to vote in the borough. He also had land elsewhere. In his will of 1803 he refers to unnamed property in Breconshire which he had agreed to sell to David Thomas for £2,900, farms in Radnorshire called 'The Cwm' and 'Blaen Kerry', land in Bettws, Disserth and Llansantffraid, several unnamed properties in Weobley, four unnamed properties in Builth Wells, and other leasehold estates. He was clearly very prosperous. Most of his property was let or sublet, but he also farmed himself, probably at Park Barn farm, where he bred cattle. After his first wife's death, he married in 1776 another Mary, possibly Mary Jones, daughter of a surgeon in Weobley. He became a church warden in Weobley and is commemorated by a wall monument immediately to the right of the altar in the church. He died in June 1809, 'at a very advanced age', according to the *Hereford Journal,* though in fact he was seventy-five. He obviously had great influence in the area, and he undoubtedly knew the Kinnersleys.

Evan Lloyd of Weobley's eldest son, another Evan, continued the social rise of the family. He was baptised at Disserth with his twin sister Mary on 19th August 1761, but grew up in Weobley, where he continued to own land or to lease it from the Marquess of Bath. His father's cousin, David Thomas, became Deputy Paymaster of the forces, and it was probably through his influence that young Evan got his first commission in the army. His career was spent in the 17th Regiment of Light Dragoons, which later became known as the 7th (Princess Royal's) Regiment of Dragoon Guards. He served in India, South America and Ireland, eventually reaching the full rank of General in 1841 when he was eighty. He was knighted in 1834. For many years he lived in Dublin, where he met his first and second wives, both widows. He married first Maria, daughter of Benjamin Burton of Burton Hall, County Carlow, widow of Michael Cox of Castletown. They had no children. After her death he married Alicia, Dowager Baroness Trimlestown, in 1814, and they had two daughters and a son. Alicia was the second daughter of Lieutenant-General Charles Eustace, and in 1797 had become the second wife of Nicholas Barnewall, 14th Baron Trimlestown, who died in 1813. So she was related to the titled Irish families of Eustace and Burton.

Like the Sprotts before them, the Lloyds were very conscious of their lineage and family connections. Family pedigrees were important for providing evidence for claims on land or estates. As the historian David Hey remarks, 'it paid to know who one's ancestors were in an age when claims at law were pursued unscrupulously'.[121] But by now it was more a question of social prestige. No doubt this Evan Lloyd was anxious to prove to his wife that she had not married beneath her. By marrying well, the Lloyds had allied themselves with some of the oldest families in Wales and Ireland, but the General and his wife were anxious to go beyond that. The Lloyds were given an entry in the first edition of Burke's *History of the Commoners of Great Britain and Ireland* (1838), but a good deal of the information there is inaccurate. Like many families in the nineteenth century, they claimed descent not just from Prince Llewellyn the Great, but also from English, Irish and French royalty. They suggested that they had descent connections with the Mortimers, Edward III, Edward IV and Richard III, and, even further back, with King John, the Viking King Sitric of Dublin, Charlemagne the Holy Roman Emperor, and King Arthur. The absurdity of these pedigrees is obvious. Very many socially ambitious families also applied for the grant of a coat of arms. In 1868 the College of Arms received forty-three thousand applications, most of which were spurious.[122] The General's claim of a grant of arms also turned out to be without foundation.

Towards the end of his life, he and his wife moved back to Shropshire and lived at Ferney Hall near Clungunford, where they are buried. They played a full part in Ludlow society and, unusually, the General's wife always appeared under her previous title. In December 1841, a public ball to celebrate the birth of the Prince of Wales took place at the New Rooms (the present Assembly Rooms). On the advertisement for this event there is

LUDLOW.

A PUBLIC BALL,

IN

CELEBRATION OF THE BIRTH OF THE PRINCE OF WALES.

WILL TAKE PLACE

IN THE NEW ROOMS,

ON TUESDAY, THE 21st OF DECEMBER, 1841.

PATRONESSES.	PATRONS.
The Right Hon. The Countess of Powis	The Right Hon. The Earl of Powis
The Lady Harriet Clive	The Hon. R. H. Clive, M. P.
The Lady Trimlestown	The Hon. G. F. Hamilton
The Hon. Mrs. Hamilton	Sir W. E. Rouse Boughton, Bart.
Lady Rouse Boughton	Sir Charles Cuyler, Bart.
Lady Syer	General Sir Evan Lloyd
Lady Cuyler	Sir Edward Thomason, Knight
Lady Thomason	Le Comte de Croismare
Mrs. Ackers	James Ackers, Esq. M. P.
Mrs. Botfield	B. Botfield, Esq. M. P.
Mrs. Bridges	Thomas Botfield, Esq.
Mrs. Dunne	T. C. Bridges, Esq.
Mrs. Hutchings	Thomas Dunne, Esq.
Mrs. Rogers	Henry Hallifax, Esq.
Mrs. Russell	John Hutchings, Esq.
Mrs. Salwey	Edward Rogers, Esq.
Mrs. Wakefield	General Russell
	John Salwey, Esq.
	R. Wakefield, Esq., Mayor

STEWARDS.

Mr. Anderson	Mr. Alderman Harding
Mr. R. Anderson	Mr. Hotchkiss
Mr. Baxter	Mr. W. Lloyd
Dr. Bryce	Mr. Marston
Mr. Childe	Mr. Massey
Mr. J. Cooper	Mr. G. Morris
Mr. Downes	Mr. H. Salwey
Mr. W. Edwards, jun.	Mr. J. C. Smith
Mr. Grounds	Dr. Stocker

The proceeds of the Ball will be added to the Subscription for providing the Poor with Fuel, Food, and Clothing.

TICKETS.—Ladies 4s., Gentlemen 5s 6d. (including Tea and Coffee), to be had at the Booksellers, or of J. HEATON, the Library, Public Rooms.

A Supper will be provided, Tickets (optional), 2s. 6d.—Dancing to commence at Nine o'Clock.

Ludlow, December 7th, 1841.

R. Jones, Printer, Broad Street, Ludlow.

38. A NOTICE OF THE BALL TO CELEBRATE THE BIRTH OF THE PRINCE OF WALES
in which Alicia, Lady Trimelstown, and her husband, the General, feature prominently

a list in order of rank of the Patrons, Patronesses and Stewards, drawn from the cream of Ludlow society. Among the Patronesses, Lady Trimlestown, keeping her previous married name, appears high on the list, with only the Right Hon. The Countess of Powis and Lady Harriet Clive above her. The General himself is sixth on the list of Patrons, and his nephew, William, is among the Stewards.

After the General's death in 1846, his widow spent her last years at Fishmore Hall, nearer the town, until she died in 1860. As a widow, she continued to maintain her position in Ludlow society, appearing again as a patron of the ball to celebrate the opening of the railway in 1852. Her son, Captain Lloyd, is also mentioned. After her death, Fishmore Hall was lived in from 1863 to 1873 by Rev. Arthur Pardoe, the son of Ellen Sneade and George Dansey Pardoe.

Of the remaining sons of Evan Lloyd of Weobley, John was a soldier and died young in Jamaica in 1795, while Thomas became a clergyman. By the time he died in 1822, he was vicar of Eaton-under-Heywood, a living in the gift of his brothers, Henry and William. These two brothers, born in 1766 and 1773, both became attorneys. From at least 1795 they practised in Ludlow, together at first, though when William married Anne Preece, his niece's sister-in-law and daughter of William Preece of Yatton, Aymestrey, he joined the Preece practice in Leominster, but continued to live in Ludlow. Henry and William already had strong associations with the Sprott family, having acted as executors or trustees for Thomas Yate of Ashford Carbonel, who had inherited the Sprott estate, and then for his son, Samuel Yate Sprott. They also acted for Lucy Kinnersley.

Henry married Thomasin Eaton from Leominster in 1795 when they were both aged twenty-nine, and in that year they are recorded as living in St Leonard's House, at the top of Upper Linney. In 1758 this building had been a stable and garden; by 1775 it was a 'messuage', and by 1786 it had become a 'new erected house adjoining Linney Gate'. After he moved to the Broad

39. PORTRAITS OF HENRY AND THOMASIN LLOYD
Thomasin is wearing the ring shown in Fig.27

Gate in 1815, Henry continued to lease the house from the Corporation, but sublet it. When his father died, he took over the post of bailiff for the Marquess of Bath's estates in Weobley and Minsterley, and, like his brothers, leased land in Weobley.

Evan's will had stipulated that his freehold and leasehold land should be sold and the money distributed among his children, apart from his eldest son, Evan, whom he had 'already amply provided for'. But Henry seems to have come to some arrangement with his brothers to take over his father's leases, including Park Barn. In a survey of vicarial tithes for 1826 it is said that 'Mr Henry Lloyd of Ludlow took over all his father's land'. In the register of electors for Weobley in the 1830s, his place of abode is Ludlow, but his voting qualification is a 'messuage, farm and lands in my own occupation' in Weobley. Park Barn Farm, which was, at one point occupied by his brothers, was leasehold, but Henry had bought a considerable amount of freehold land between Park Barn and the village itself, together with land at Weobley Marsh. General Sir Evan Lloyd and his brother, William, also appear to have owned land in the area. In all, Henry farmed two hundred and forty acres and bred Hereford cattle. He is reported to have bred a prize bull, 'Chancellor', on his farm at Weobley, 'which bull was a pure Knight bull from a Tomkins cow' (Tomkins was the founder of the Hereford breed.)[123] He also managed to be a successful solicitor in Ludlow. His land in Weobley passed to his son, John, after 1834, but John's second wife, who was left with seven young children, seems to have disposed of it.

When Thomasin died in 1814, and Henry had moved his family to the Broad Gate, he lived with his sister and some of the younger children, the youngest of whom, Sarah, was ten. The Lloyds leased or owned the Broad Gate for one hundred and thirty two years thereafter, from 1814 to 1946. In 1822 Pigot's Directory describes Henry and William as practising from somewhere near the churchyard, probably St Leonard's House, as it was usual at the time for trades and professions to be practised from home. At the early-nineteenth-century bank, Rocke, Eyton & Co., based in the fine Georgian house at 18, Broad Street, the managers did not just live on the premises, but had their own front door, which rather destroys the symmetry of the house. The banker and lawyer, James Kinnersley, may well have run his business from the Broad Gate itself. Doctors and dentists continued to practise from their own houses well into the twentieth century, but, with the great increase of business, lawyers needed designated offices, and the Lloyds decided that they needed purpose-built chambers.

On the south side of the western tower of the Broad Gate, the house, which was part of the estate, was now demolished and replaced by a three-storey

40. VIEWS OF THE BROAD GATE FROM THE SOUTH
(above) before the chambers were built, in Thomas Gregory's Shropshire Gazetteer *of 1824,*
and (right) in Henry Ziegler's view of 1826, after their construction.
Ziegler shows the post horn being blown to signal arrival

building in the neo-Gothick style intended to echo, and, indeed, to expand on the style of the northern frontage. A two-storey battlemented extension was added to it, running west into the yard. The date for the building must be somewhere between 1824, when it is missing from an engraving in Gregory's 'Directory', and 1826, when it appears in Henry Ziegler's water-colour of Lower Broad Street.

The design of the new building tells us something about Henry Lloyd. He took the Gothick castellated theme of the eighteenth-century north front and elaborated it even further with a medieval tower, a hanging turret on the corner, indented decoration to the wall, and, most strikingly, three large windows 'with pretty Gothick trim',[124] one above the other. Inside each

of the three rooms built against the tower, the convex wall still remains. Although some of the architectural ornaments have disappeared, including the western extension, the new building is still one of great charm and romance, a kind of enlarged Wemmick's castle in its playfulness, but, like Samuel Sprott, Henry Lloyd was also making a serious statement about the status and ancient origin of his family.

He may have been able to extend the Broad Gate in this way because of the security offered by the Corporation in their granting of leaseholds. Leases generally ran for thirty-one years, but since 1690 the arrangement was that, after twenty-four years, leaseholders could renew their leases at the same rent. If they did not do so, they paid a tax or 'fine' for each year remaining on the lease. In 1724 John Stead had had to pay a fine for not petitioning for a new lease, though the interest was remitted 'on account of the house being burnt and his rebuilding same'. It was, therefore, very much to the advantage of the lessee to petition early for a new lease. This system meant that the lease was more like a freehold. Lessees could treat the property as if they owned it, and could sublet and 'alien' the lease. It also meant that they could improve or extend their properties quite freely. Just as John Stead could build his house as he pleased over the Broad Gate, so Henry Lloyd could extend it beyond the towers to accommodate his legal practice.

The building of the new chambers was probably the reason for throwing together two of the three ground floor parlours in the main house. The resulting larger room became a drawing room overlooking the garden, as well as Broad Street. Because the hill rises so steeply, the third storey of the new building is on the same level as the 'ground' floor of the main house. This top room appears to have been a library for Henry's fine collection of law books. The later Lloyds used it as their informal family sitting-room, connected as it was to the main house, but it was always known as the 'library'. With its windows on three sides and its eminence on the hill, it gives fine views of the countryside around. It was not directly accessible from the legal chambers below, though there may have been an entrance from the staircase leading to the west cellar into the second floor room, which, with its larger window, was probably the office of the main partner of the firm, Henry himself. In the twentieth century this room became his great-grand-daughter's sitting-room. The rooms for the clerks were in the further battlemented extension to the west. One of them, Jacob Huxley, who died in 1839, is described as the confidential clerk of the late Henry Lloyd Esq., solicitor, Ludlow. He appears to have lived or owned property in Lower Raven Lane. Outside the house, in front of the ground floor window, were elegant railings, designed to match the stonework over the windows above. There were also imposing solid gates into the back yard.

Pigot's trade directory for Ludlow in 1828 shows that Henry Lloyd and his brother William were still practising from the 'churchyard', but in the same year Tibnam's directory shows Henry and his two sons, John and William, now installed at the Broad Gate. Henry remained there until his death in 1834 and John was still there in Slater's directory for 1850. William had died in 1843 and his son, Robert, joined his uncle as an articled clerk by 1851. He was a partner by 1861, but shortly afterwards was based at 9 Castle Street in the practice of Southern, Appleton and Lloyd, where the practice continued after John's death in 1869. The Broad Gate chambers were probably too far away from the centre of town. The Lloyds seem to have used the extra rooms in the new building for storage, and so they remained until after the Second World War.

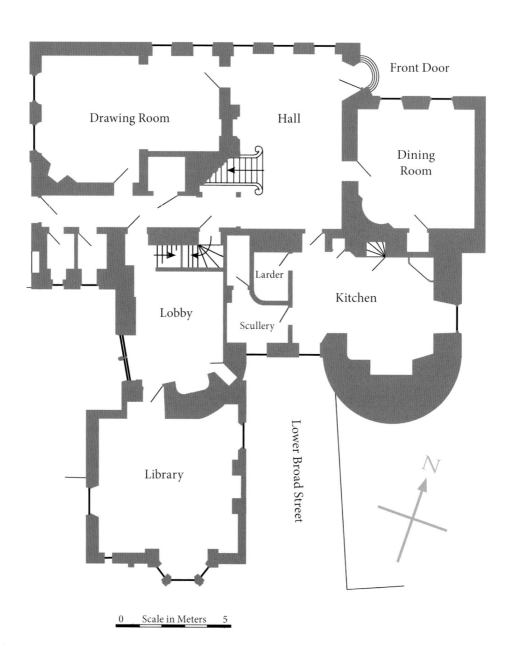

Front Door

Drawing Room

Hall

Dining Room

Larder

Lobby

Scullery

Kitchen

Library

Lower Broad Street

N

0   Scale in Meters   5

A GROUND FLOOR PLAN OF THE LLOYD HOUSE

− 8 −

THE LLOYDS II

Earlier in the eighteenth century, before the Kinnersleys and the Lloyds began to practise, the distinction between different legal practitioners had been similar to that between those in medicine. Attorneys (increasingly called 'solicitors') and barristers were distinguished from each other in the same way as surgeons and physicians. Barristers graduated from the inns of court; attorneys were apprenticed or belonged to the Inns of Chancery, which were subordinate to the Inns of Court. There was the same difference in social origin and status. Barristers were titled 'Esquire'; attorneys were merely 'Gentlemen'. Barristers were trained in the theoretical principles of law, and appeared before the highest courts of the land; attorneys acted in the Court of Common Pleas and applied the law to the practical day-to-day needs of clients.

Like doctors, lawyers of all kinds had very often been regarded as parasites, knaves or impostors, only out to exploit people, but, as legal issues became more complicated and legal expertise more necessary, attorneys as well as barristers strove to control their profession and to regulate it from within. The present Law Society did not come into being until 1825, but from 1739, with the founding of the Society of Gentlemen Practitioners for the London area, and other societies in the provinces, there began a serious attempt to insist on respect for the profession, to demand the highest standards of probity from those who practised it, and to define the areas which could not be encroached upon either from below or above. In particular, it became accepted that barristers could deal with clients only through a solicitor.

In practice, barristers tended to be drawn to London and the central courts, where they could attract much higher fees than in the provinces. Solicitors in provincial towns and country areas dealt with the administration of deeds, wills, leases, conveyances, mortgages, marriage settlements, indentures, trusts and disputes. Very little of their work involved appearing in court. Some solicitors acted as agents for large estates, or as clerks for charities. As we have seen, they very often dealt in investments or loans, which led to their becoming bankers. They might hold office as Town Clerks, or fill posts under the Lord Lieutenant, such as Clerk of the Peace, a position which had been held by the younger James Kinnersley in Herefordshire.

Solicitors tended to become indispensable members of the community, entrusted with a great deal of private information and they acquired considerable local knowledge. This gave them a unique position in society. To keep it, they needed to maintain strict standards of honesty and respectability. By establishing their reputation for straight dealing, they were setting 'a certain level of behaviour for all who wished to stand well with their fellows'.[125] In the past, attorneys, even from poor backgrounds, had used their increased wealth and influence to buy the land and property without which they could not aspire to the ranks of the gentry. This was particularly so in Ludlow, where, under the Council in the Marches, lawyers had connections with London and the court, and high social ambitions. The practice of law and the acquisition of land which often followed it had always been a route to social success, but by the end of the eighteenth century, membership of the profession in itself conferred status. Attorneys did not necessarily retire to landed estates. They bought the best houses in country towns in which to live and practise, and set themselves up as an urban aristocracy. The Lloyds already had some social standing, and, with the exception of General Sir Evan Lloyd, they did not feel the need to 'marry up'. Their wives came from other legal or professional families. They were the daughters of solicitors, agents, doctors or clergymen; their daughters married into similar families, and most of their surviving sons followed them into the professions.

Henry Lloyd was a man of property. As well as leasing the Broad Gate and land in Weobley, he owned other houses in Ludlow. He and his sons were important figures in the town. Henry was elected to the Ludlow Corporation in 1830 and his sons William and Thomas in 1833. The Corporation Minutes record the bill from J. Williams, Town Clerk, to Henry Lloyd Esq., Solicitor, Ludlow, for his election as Honorary Burgess:

Town Clerk & Deputy's fee	*1. 6. 0*
3 Serjeants	*7. 6*
Bellman & Cryer	*5. 0*
3 Beadles	*4. 6*
Fine to the Corporation	*13. 4*
Stamps on Parchment	*3. 0. 6*

Similar amounts were charged by the Clerk on Henry's swearing in as a member of the Ludlow Corporation, with the addition of a Prayer Book for the Corporation Seat, costing £2. 10s, and 'a Moiety of money given to the Ringers, £1 given in Ale to the Corporation Stewards and them [the ringers], as agreed upon between Mr Lloyd & myself'. Clearly, these were grand and expensive occasions. As men of substance, Henry and his sons subscribed to funds for paving and lighting in the town in 1832. In the List of the Poll for the election of that year they were described as 'burgesses' and 'gentlemen'. Later, as between 'the Clivites and Reformers' they were supporters of the Clives, that is to say, of the establishment. In December 1835, the first municipal election was won by the Reformers. Henry's son, William, as a Tory, secured only eighty-three votes, and so was not elected a member of the new Borough Council. In the 1840 General Election, he gave his votes for the Conservatives. This political allegiance continued into the twentieth century, with John Lloyd's son, Edward Stanley, who, in November 1922, was one of eight nominators of Viscount Windsor, who was seeking re-election as a Conservative MP.

Henry's brother, the older William, who was baptised at Weobley in 1773 with his twin sister Elizabeth, at first practised as a solicitor with him at St Leonard's House. When he was twenty-five and still perhaps a law student, his letter of 1798 written from Gray's Inn to his brother is mainly concerned with legal cases they were involved in, but there are passages which shed more light on his life. He congratulates Henry and his wife Thomasin on the birth of their third son, his namesake, William:

> *I am very glad to hear Mrs Lloyd and the Children are so well. I hope she is got down Stairs. I am not a little proud of the Honour of being the young Gent.'s Godfather. I should have liked much to have been present on the occasion.*

He then describes a visit to the theatre, to see *Lovers' Vows*, the very play which is the subject of so much drama in Jane Austen's *Mansfield Park*. The play was clearly very popular, but in the novel it was a little *risqué* for the young people to be performing when Sir Thomas Bertram unexpectedly returns. William's letter relates:

> *I was at the Covent Garden Theatre on Wednesday last for seeing the new Play called* Lovers Vows *which is a very good one & much admired, but my chief object was to see the Royal Family, but it was at the Expence of a devilish hard squeezing … from the Crowd trying to get in for the same purpose, particularly as it was expected his Majesty would be received with great Acclamation on account of the late Victories [the Battle of the Nile], which was the case. We have*

*official accounts of Captain Troughbridge having taken or destroyed
all the transport at Alexandria.*

In fact, 'Captain Troughbridge', in reality Rear-admiral Sir Thomas
Troughbridge, was unable to take part in the battle itself, as his ship, the
Culloden, was stuck on a shoal and immoveable. Nelson, however, insisted
on his being awarded a gold medal to celebrate the victory. William's letter
continues with an enquiry after his brother Tom, the clergyman, who was
still seeking a living; a question about Henry's partner, Baxter, coming to
town – 'Perhaps the Balls keep him at home'; a reference to a goose sent to
Miss Eaton; and an enquiry after some tobacco sent but not acknowledged.

A good deal of business was done between London and Ludlow, and it
is remarkable how often serious letters of legal business contain thanks for
gifts of game or poultry sent up from the country. In a letter of 14th February
1789 James Kinnersley is thanked for the 'Turkey, Chine and Hare which
all was very good, and I have sent you a barrel of oysters of which I must
beg your acceptance by your next courier which I hope will prove good'. In
October 1801 it appears that William Lloyd had unfortunately left the New
Inn in London before the arrival of a letter, postmarked Ludlow, and two
parcels, 'one of which containing Game, as we suppose, we will have opened.
Mr Lloyd having left London yesterday evening, we beg to be instructed how
to dispose of these things'. One correspondent, writing to Henry Lloyd from
the Wheatsheaf (in London not Ludlow), begs him for:

*a nice hogshead of perry as I understand it is very fine this year and
as you mentioned to me you thought you could execute the same,
I now avail myself of the opportunity. You will have the goodness
to have it cased to prevent any adulteration on the road, and on its
arrival I will send you down the amount. You will let me know when
it is coming. The best conveyance is by canal.*

41. THE LUDLOW CARRIER COACH
An oil painting of 1801 by Jacques-Laurent Agasse, possibly the very coach which the Lloyds
used to send game to William in London

Apart from 'adulteration', there was always a concern for the state of the item when it arrived, which is hardly surprising given the conditions in which it travelled. A letter to Henry's son William in 1833 asks him to thank his father for 'his kind present of game, which arrived perfectly good'. This same letter, from a Mr Engelheart of Doctors' Commons, includes a bill for work done for the Lloyds on the probate of a will. It gives an idea of the complexity of such work and the cost involved.

IN THE GOODS OF JAMES GWILLIAM DECEASED 1833 13th SEPTEMBER

Praying a Commission to swear the Executors of the Will			
of the deceased & paid surrogates fee		7.	0
Warrant to lead the Commission & Stamp thereon		7.	0
Commission (with Blank) under Seal and Stamp		16.	10
Extracting same		6.	0
Drawing & engrossing an Affidavit to be made by			
the Executors for the Commissioners of Stamps		6.	0
Certificate of Execution, and Instructions		3.	4
Returning the Commission and praying Probate		6.	0
Paid filing the Affidavit & Attendance thereon		10.	2
Engrossing the Will for Probate and paid for			
registering the same and collating	9.	10.	10
Probate under Seal and Stamp	131.	18.	2
Extracting the same		13.	4
Clerks and Parchment	1.	7.	6
Postage and Carriage		4.	2

The total was £146.19.8, which was a huge sum. It is not difficult to see how lawyers made their money.[126]

After the elder William Lloyd's marriage to Anne Preece in 1800, he worked in the Leominster chambers of her father, William Preece. Her brother married William's niece, Maria Poppleton, daughter of his sister Anne, so the families became even more closely related. William Lloyd, his wife and eight children lived in Ludlow, from 1807 to 1815 at 56 Mill Street. Both brothers appear to have had an interest in Ludlow Grammar School, as they signed a petition in 1808 to remove the headmaster, even though William's eldest son was still a baby and at least one of Henry's sons, John, went to Shrewsbury School from 1811. John Lloyd's sons, Henry's grandsons, almost certainly attended the Grammar School, though Edward Stanley, the youngest son, spent a year at Shrewsbury. In March, 1881, George Frederick, the middle son, appears in a published list of those at Ludlow Grammar School who had passed Class III in the Cambridge Local Examinations. We do not know whether the daughters went to school, and if so, where, though there were plenty of ladies' academies in Ludlow throughout the eighteenth and nineteenth centuries.

As the *Salopian Journal* for 2nd October 1822 reported, William himself died unexpectedly on 22nd September while staying at Pontarddulais near Swansea:

> *To the inexpressible grief of his afflicted family, William Lloyd, Esq., solicitor of Ludlow. His conciliatory manner and inflexible integrity had justly gained the lasting regard of many valuable friends, who will long and sincerely regret his premature death.*

Like his father, his brother and his sister-in-law, William has a memorial in Weobley parish church, although he was buried with his wife's family at Aymestrey. His branch of the Lloyds inherited the solicitors' firm from William Preece, and continued to practise in Leominster for another four generations, until 1965.

According to the Easter book of 1816, the widowed Henry Lloyd was residing at the Broad Gate, and had been joined by one of his sisters, no doubt to look after his younger children. Of his four daughters, Mary, Anne, Caroline and Sarah, only Sarah married. Her husband was Henry Hodges, a doctor, known locally as 'the poor man's friend'.[127] His sister, Charlotte Hodges, married Sarah's brother, John, yet another example of the interconnectedness of local families. The boys were Henry, John, William and Thomas. In 1818 or 1819 their father married a second wife, Anne Harriet ('Nerry') Lewis. This was to be the first of two connections with the Lewis family. Henry and Nerry had no children themselves, and after 1832 the Easter Books describe him as living alone at the Broad Gate with one of his daughters by his first marriage. This would have been either Anne

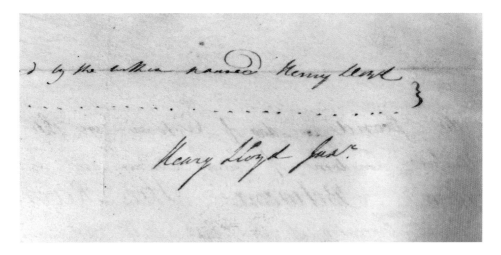

42. HENRY LLOYD JUNIOR'S SIGNATURE
as a witness on the conveyance to his father of the lease of the Broad Gate in 1815

(1800-68) or Caroline (1803-53), since his eldest daughter, Mary (b. 1796) had died in May 1831, and Sarah had married. There were also a man and three maids, but no mention of Henry's wife Nerry, although she did not die until December 6th 1839. Unlike Henry and his first wife, Thomasin, who have a memorial in Weobley church, she is buried in the churchyard at St Giles, Ludford.

Like Samuel Sprott's supposed son William (see p. 70), Henry's eldest son, another Henry, is a man of mystery. The conveyance drawn up in 1815, when George Dansey Pardoe transferred the lease of the Broad Gate to Henry Lloyd, was witnessed by Henry Lloyd Junior. He would have been twenty at the time. Thereafter his association with the family seems to have been broken. In the 1851 census he is entered as a lodger at 31 Lower Broad Street. He gives his age as fifty-five, says that he was born in Ludlow, that he is married and that he is a solicitor, but he does not appear as a solicitor in the records of the Law Society. He also seems not to have been mentioned in any will or Letters of Administration, although there is a record in the Ludlow parish register of a Henry Lloyd who married Mary Cadona in 1821. Various addresses are given for 'Henry Lloyd' in the town in later censuses, and he may have been the Henry Lloyd who died in Ludlow in 1859. There seems to have been a falling-out with his father, as he does not appear in Henry senior's will of 1834. The second and third sons, John and William, followed their father into the law. In 1834 they were executors of his will and paid a rent of £1.18s to the Corporation for the lease of the Broad Gate.

The three Lloyd brothers, John, William and Thomas were important members of Ludlow society, but it is clear that William and Thomas (when he was around) were much more active in Ludlow affairs than John. William and Thomas were burgesses, and it is William who was on many committees and involved in local politics, and Thomas who chaired meetings in the town. John's name rarely appears, although he was involved in the creation of the new Assembly Rooms, of which he was a shareholder. After his father's death, he and his wife, Charlotte, moved from 15 Corve Street into the Broad Gate around 1835; the 1841 census shows them, both aged forty, living there. They had no children. In 1843, the rate book cites John Lloyd as the owner, i.e. the leaseholder, of the Broad Gate, but mentions his brother, William, as an occupier, probably sharing the legal chambers. The house, garden, stables and grounds (1 acre, 16 perches) are valued at £49, and the chambers at £14.

William the younger and his family resided first at 56 Mill Street and then at 15 Broad Street, where they lived with his uncle William's widow, Anne Lloyd. On 11th June 1838 they were involved in what might have been a serious accident. The *Salopian Journal* records that William with his children and their governess were returning from a drive over Maryknoll, when their horse ran away and 'went down a steep declivity to Whitcliffe Coppice at the Bowling Green Gate at the entrance to the coppice'. The horse was killed, but everyone else survived.

Like his namesake uncle and godfather, William did not live long. He was only forty-five when he died in 1843 of what seems to have been either heart failure or a pulmonary embolism. On 28th February 1844 the *Hereford Journal* advertised a four-day sale of 'Valuable and Handsome Furniture' of the late Mr William Lloyd. The sale included the whole of the household furniture, china, glass, plate, bed and table linen. An 'excellent' mangle is singled out for special mention, as is a 'four wheel carriage, gig and harness'. As with other members of his family, he had invested in property in Ludlow, some in Weeping Cross Lane. 14 Broad Street belonged to him in 1843.

William had married Frances Tench, daughter of Robert Tench, land-agent, of Bromfield. She had died in 1838, possibly in childbirth, as her baby daughter died in 1841, when she was three years old. Her sister Lydia married William's brother Thomas. William and Frances had five children. The eldest daughter, Frances, married Francis Southern, solicitor, one of the partners of Southern, Lloyd and Appleton.[128] Frances, or Fanny, corresponded with Thomas Wright (1810-1877), the distinguished Ludlow historian and antiquarian. She collected autographs, but Wright seems to have regarded her as a serious correspondent, as he sent her a proof of his history of Fulk Fitz-Warine. When Fanny died of cancer in 1861, her husband kept Wright's letters and her collection of autographs.[129] He and Fanny had lived at 31 Broad Street, a stone's throw from the Broad Gate. Of her three brothers, Charles died at eighteen, Herbert emigrated to Philadelphia, and Robert became a solicitor like his father. In the 1851 census he appears as an articled clerk aged eighteen living with his uncle, John Lloyd, at the Broad Gate. By 1861 he was working with him at the Broad Gate chambers. He married Eliza Lightbody in 1871, but died the following year of kidney disease, aged thirty-nine.

Henry Lloyd's youngest son, Thomas, was born in 1802. Following his brother William, he married another daughter of Robert Tench, Lydia, but they were married far from Ludlow, in Childwall, Lancashire. They had two sons. The elder, Thomas Evan Lloyd, born in 1845, emigrated with his family to Australia around 1889. He became assistant town clerk at St. Kilda, near Melbourne, and then in 1891 Secretary of the Shire of Yarrawonga, Victoria. In 1893, however, he was sentenced to eighteen months hard labour for embezzlement. His family returned to England without him, and he died in 1909 at Braidwood, New South Wales, where he was working as a nurseryman. One of his sons, Edward Francis Lloyd, worked for Lloyds of London. The second son of Thomas, Robert Henry Lloyd, emigrated to America and little is known about him.

Dr Thomas Lloyd himself is perhaps the most interesting of the Lloyds. He graduated with a medical degree from Edinburgh at the age of twenty four in 1826, but in 1822 he was studying anatomy in Bristol, apprenticed to a Mr Edgill. A photocopy survives of a letter from Thomas to his father, Henry. It begins, like many letters from twenty-year-olds, with a request for money, but develops into something rather surprising:

Bristol Nov. 25th 1822

Dear Father

I am very sorry to trouble you again on the subject of my pockets, but they are so low that I am obliged to remind you of it – and, if convenient, I should be thankful if you could remit some money by return of post.

I am on excellent terms with Mr. Edgill and his family, therefore shall think that the petition upon the Infirmary business would be successful. Mr. E. told me this morning that he expected another Apprentice, the son of a Clergyman in [ ]. I trust this may be true but am afraid that upon further enquiries the young gentleman will be [ ] We are sadly off for subjects this Winter, almost every attempt to procure them having been unsuccessful. One half of our pupils are now under prosecution for the attempt. I was fortunate enough to get one Friday last, after working six hours, for they bury them in all the Churches the depth of six feet, so that we were literally obliged to help each other in getting out of the grave. I was assisted by one young man only.

I do not intend going out again unless circumstances are very pressing. The fatigue is too much. In London subjects are so scarce that 25 Gns are offered for one. Indeed it is said that there is but one Anatomist there who can procure them at any rate. In the Dublin schools they are procured eight and forty hours only after death for five shillings.

With kind regards to all at home
I remain D[ea]r Father
In haste
your Affect[ionate]
Th Lloyd[130]

Only a month earlier *The Bristol Journal* of 26th October 1822 had reported that a body had been snatched from the churchyard at St Augustine's church and taken to a dissecting room hired by some Bristol surgeons in the precincts of the Cathedral. There had been a quarrel between the surgeons and the 'resurrection men', no doubt over their fee, and they had been discovered. It was not a crime to disinter bodies until the 1850s, as they were thought to have no legal rights and to belong to no-one, but it was illegal to steal anything from a grave, so the corpse was removed naked, the coffin and shroud being left behind. It was a crime, however, to dissect bodies other than those of executed criminals.

Anatomy had advanced rapidly since the days of Doctors Stead and Sprott. Brilliant surgeons such as William Hunter (1718-1783), the famous anatomist and obstetrician, and his brother John (1728-1793), and those at the advanced medical schools in Edinburgh, inspired a great expansion in the profession. In 1747 R. Campbell in *The London Tradesman* had insisted that a surgeon 'must be an accurate anatomist. It is not sufficient for him

43. *DR THOMAS LLOYD 1802–1849*
was an enthusiastic amateur geologist

to attend anatomical lectures, but he must put his hand to it himself'.[131] Anatomists needed corpses, or what Thomas calls 'subjects', and far more than could be supplied legally. Commercial body-snatchers filled the gap and preyed on town and village graveyards. The Anatomy Act of 1832, in the face of furious opposition, put a stop to the activities of the body-snatchers by giving the anatomists legal access to bodies that were unclaimed after death, which meant generally those who died in workhouses, charity hospitals or prisons. In 1822 Thomas and his friends clearly could not afford what was charged by the 'resurrectionists', and took it into their own hands to find corpses for the dissecting table. His letter gives a glimpse of a very different world. One wonders what his father, the lawyer, would have thought of it all.

After qualifying at Edinburgh, Thomas spent three years as an assistant surgeon in Bombay from 1827 to 1830 and then returned as Senior Physician at the Ludlow Dispensary for the next twelve years. While he lived in Ludlow, he leased 19 Broad Street from the Corporation. Apart from his medical practice, he was also known as an enthusiastic geologist. At this time there was a great interest in mapping the geological strata of the whole of the British Isles, pioneered by William Smith, who had published the first geological map of England, Wales and Scotland in 1815, but continued by numerous amateur geologists throughout the country. In 1831 one of the most important contemporary geologists, Roderick Impey Murchison (1792-1871), who identified the Silurian System, was travelling in South Wales and the Marches, looking at rocks in the 'transition period'. While he was there, he met Thomas Taylor Lewis, the curate at Aymestrey, near Wigmore. Lewis was an antiquary who edited the letters of Brilliana Harley, but he was also a geologist. He persuaded Murchison of the importance of the Ludlow area in his researches, and, through him, Murchison met Thomas Lloyd in 1832. Along with the work of seven or eight other local naturalists, Thomas Lloyd's research was sent through Lewis to Murchison, whose discoveries inspired a passion in these young geologists. 'I am still warm with the enthusiasm I caught from you,' Thomas Lloyd wrote later to Murchison, who regarded Lewis and Lloyd as 'my friends and excellent Ludlow coadjutors'.

In November 1832 Dr Lloyd made an important discovery. He found fossil fragments in the local red sandstone, which before had been thought to be unfossiliferous. These fragments, which at first were believed to be crustaceous, were later identified as some of the oldest fish known at that time. Another important find was his discovery in 1834 of the 'ginger-coloured' rock in the quarry by Ludford Bridge, nowadays known as the Ludlow bone bed. The fossils here were at that time the oldest known vertebrate remains. Murchison's book *Silurian System,* published in 1839, and his later volume of 1854, *Siluria*, acknowledge the assistance of Lloyd and his fellow geologists. The new species of fossils included *Pleurotomaria Lloydii* and *Trinucleus Lloydii*.[132]

Thomas Lloyd and Thomas Taylor Lewis were both on the first committee of the Ludlow Natural History Society which founded the Ludlow Museum in 1833; and, later, Thomas Lloyd was made the Museum's honorary curator. The Society itself lasted until the 1920s. Dr Lloyd moved to Aberystwyth, perhaps for his health, as he died there at Marine Terrace of heart disease in 1849, aged forty-seven.

ROYAL MAILS

AND

FAST POST COACHES,

FROM THE

Swan Hotel, Birmingham.

	MORNING.	EVENING.
LONDON TALLY-HO! thro' Coventry in 11 hours	 8	
LONDON—Day, thro' Oxford	.. ½ past 10	
LONDON—Royal Mail	.. ..	 6
LONDON—Greyhound	.. ..	 7
LONDON—Express	.. ¼ before 5	
ALCESTER and REDDITCH	 7	
BANBURY	 7	
BATH	 9	
BRISTOL	.. ½ before 7	
BEWDLEY	.. 8 and 9	
CHELTENHAM and GLOUCESTER ..	.. 7 9, and 12	
CARLISLE and LAN- CASTER	.. 6 and 7	8 and ½ past 9
COVENTRY	 8	2, 5, 6, and 7
DERBY	.. 6 and 10	
DUDLEY	.. 8 and 9	.. ½ past 4
EDINBURGH ½ before 6 and ½ before 7		8 and ½ past 9
GLASGOW ½ before 6 and ½ before 7		8 and ½ past 9
HOLYHEAD & DUBLIN Royal Mail............	.. 8 and 10	
KIDDERMINSTER ..	.. 8 and 9	.. ½ past 4
LEEDS	.. 6 and 10	
LEICESTER	 8	.. ½ past 2
LIVERPOOL ..	7 and ½ past 8	8 and ½ past 9
LEAMINGTON ..	5, 7, and ½ past 10	 5
LICHFIELD ..	6, 7, and 10	 4
LUDLOW and CLEOBURY ..	9	
MANCHESTER ½ before 6 and ½ before 7		8 and ½ past 9
NOTTINGHAM ..	6, 8, and 10	
OXFORD—Day ..	.. ½ past 10	
POTTERIES ..	 7	
RUDGLEY ..	 7	 4
SHEFFIELD ..	6 and 10	
STAMFORD—Royal Mail	.. 8	
STOURPORT—Royal Mail	.. 8	
SHREWSBURY ..	.. 8 and 10	
STOURBRIDGE ..	.. 8 and 9	.. ½ past 4
WARWICK .. 5, 7, and ½ past 10		 5
WORCESTER ..	7, 9, and 12	.. ½ past 3
WOLVERHAMPTON	6, 7, 8, and 10	.. 4, 8 and 9

THOS. WADDELL,

PROPRIETOR.

FLIES, CARS, &c.

Always ready for the accommodation of Passengers.

44. AN 1835 STAGE COACH TIMETABLE FROM BIRMINGHAM
with departures to Ludlow and Cleobury leaving at 9 am each day

− 9 −

NINETEENTH-CENTURY LUDLOW

Important changes were taking place in Broad Street in Henry Lloyd's time at the Broad Gate. At the end of the eighteenth century, in 1795, cast iron had replaced the wooden posts supporting Butcher's Row. A water engine had been installed in Mill Street by 1808, and gas had arrived by 1830. In April 1821 there was a general meeting of the inhabitants of Ludlow to discuss a parliamentary bill for paving the footpaths in the town. In October 1826 the Corporation gave permission for Broad Street to be pitched or macadamized; and in 1827 it was decided to pave the area under the Broad Gate with flagstones called 'Scotch pavement'. Most important was the alteration to the street level. As early as 1748, the Corporation had been improving the road at Ludford Bridge, 'for making a sufficient road for wheel carriages to pass by there and go up the Olde Street instead of the Broad Street', but, as we have seen, their scheme for removing the Broad Gate in 1792 had come to nothing. Stage coaches coming from the Crown or the Angel still had to negotiate the archway under the house, and by 1828 the fashion for larger carriages meant that the steepness of the gradient had become a problem.

On 28th October that year, a petition was signed by fifty-six residents of Broad Street. They wrote that they were aware that Ludlow Corporation was intending to 'break up the surface of the said street in order to macadamise and otherwise improve the same', and that 'your Petitioners at the present time are much inconvenienced from the want of a Common Sewer in Broad Street, owing to the present Culvert being greatly out of Repair, and considerably too small for the necessary purposes of carrying off the water from the various sources'. The culvert which John Stead had been given leave to build in 1690 was clearly no longer adequate. The petitioners suggested that it would be beneficial if, at the same time as the work on the road, 'a culvert of proper dimensions was made along the centre of the said Street'. An agreement with the Corporation was signed on the same day, and Mr William Harding, who leased the Wheatsheaf, agreed to give up part of his cellars, so long as the Corporation built 'a wall sufficiently thick and strong' to prevent water entering.[133] The section taken over by the Corporation had been built in the 1300s as part of the bridge over the ditch.

The famous engineer, Thomas Telford (1757-1834), now a 'frail old man' of seventy-two, was asked by the Corporation for a solution. As a young man he had worked in Shrewsbury and been appointed the surveyor of public works in Shropshire. In 1794 he gave the Ludlow Corporation advice on the approach to Dinham Bridge and provided plans for the rebuilding of the Old Street mills in 1810, so it is not surprising that he was approached again. Telford's plan 'to render the street as uniformly easy as possible' was to 'excavate the Cavity above the Archway two

45. THOMAS TELFORD
The engineer in his earlier days

feet at the deepest part, gradually diminishing to nothing both upwards and downward'. The excavated soil was 'to be carried to and deposited on the lowest part between the Gateway and the Bridge in an easy manner'. A retaining wall was to be built to preserve the pavement outside the Lower Broad Street houses. It was estimated that the street here would be raised by four feet at the highest point. A new road surface was to be laid so as to create a steady gradient along the whole length of the hill from the river to the top of Broad Street. Brand Lane and Bell Lane were to be re-profiled on to Broad Street and the surface was to be 'finished with a coating of well-broken stone twelve inches thick with proper side drains, down which the water will run and be conveyed into the Common Sewer'.

In order to avoid any further problems with culverts, it was recommended that a 'sewer' (i.e. a storm drain) should be installed. Roadside drainage and cast iron gratings were to be provided at the same time, so that water would flow into a new drain. This new sewer was to go down the middle of the street to the river. The underground section was to be several feet high, with side walls and arch made from flat-bedded rubble stone laid in lime mortar. The estimate for constructing the sewer and connecting the drains was £459.17s.

In February 1830, Ludlow Corporation sent a note to the owners of the houses in the street, advising them that 'all persons who are desirous of having their drains made to empty into the common sewer now forming in Broad Street, should cause it to be done immediately in order to prevent the surface of the street from being again broken up'. In July Matthew Stead quoted for building the storm drain and re-profiling the street. His specification included 'the Sewer, to commence at the River at the bottom of lower Broad Street and to be continued from thence to the top of the upper Broad Street … On each side of the upper Broad Street there is to be four cross drains with proper iron gates to receive and convey the surface water into the sewer … and to be four holes left in the crown of the sewer to admit persons in when necessary … The convexity of the upper Broad

Street above the Arch way to be lowered two feet in the deepest part … The whole of the said work to be done in a substantial and workmanlike manner in all respects agreeable to this specification and to the drawings hereunto annexed and to the satisfaction of the Surveyor for the sum of £1,141. 7s 6d'.

Perhaps the residents of Broad Street were not taking their responsibilities seriously enough, as in August 1830 the Corporation sent another note: 'It is the request of the Corporation that all persons who wish to put their drains into the Main Sewer should do so immediately.' The work was duly carried out by the Steads, and the sides of the trench were later covered with the cobbles we see today. The area under the arch itself was raised a few feet, which accounts for the lowered height of the blocked-up entrance into the western tower, and the door and window into Chandler's Cottage on the east side under the arch.[134]

These improvements did not greatly affect the Broad Gate itself, where the raised bank and retaining wall leading to the front door of the house were already in existence. But the gateway was still in the way of further improvements. In his letter to the Corporation of 11th December 1829, Telford himself regretted 'that the Old Archway which divides the Upper from the Lower Broad Street, from various local Circumstances, cannot at present be altered', but he admitted that accidents very seldom occurred there and little inconvenience was experienced. According to Henry Weyman, solicitor, mayor and local historian, all the seven main gates were standing in 1726, but by 1794, all but the Broad Gate had gone.[135] The west half of Old Gate had been demolished by 1780, though the eastern tower remained as part of the Mughouse Inn until the building of Friars' Terrace in 1822. The survival of the Broad Gate was partly because there was an alternative route into town via Old Street, which, if longer, was easier to ascend, but, just as in 1792 James Kinnersley had saved the building, this time it was probably the influence of the Lloyd family that prevented the removal of the last remaining gate in the town walls, and we have them to thank for the

46. A VIEW OF BROAD STREET IN THE 1890S, ALMOST EMPTY OF TRAFFIC

existence of the house today. Even so, a plan by the Corporation in 1831 to replace Ludford Bridge and improve the southern entrance into the town might well have led to the Broad Gate's demolition. Its status as an Ancient Monument and Grade 1 Listed Building should make it safe today, but it is interesting that in the 1990s a candidate for the Ludlow Town Council proposed that the Broad Gate be pulled down to give buses and lorries a more direct route into the town centre.

Henry Lloyd died in 1834. In disposing of his estate, his first concern was his library:

I give and bequeath unto my two sons, John Lloyd and William Lloyd, all the books which shall be or belong to my Law Library at my dwelling house at Broad Gate Ludlow at the time of my decease, also the book cases, books and other furniture and other effects now in the offices occupied by me jointly with them to and for their own use absolutely.

They and his youngest son, Thomas, were named as executors who were to sell his remaining land and property, dividing the proceeds between them, with a bequest of £1,000 to each of the three surviving daughters 'for their separate use'.

By 1835 John Lloyd, Henry's second son, had moved into the Broad Gate. He was now, in the absence of his older brother, Henry, the head of the family, and senior partner in the solicitors' firm. He inherited the Broad Gate lease and, with his brother William, built up the estate by buying 4 and 5 High Street and 73 and 74 Lower Broad Street. They still leased St Leonard's House and the nearby stable, as well as farming considerable amounts of land at Weobley. After William's death in 1843, John worked alone at the Broad Gate, until he was joined by his nephew, Robert.

Robert continued to practise at the Broad Gate, and then at chambers with Francis Southern in 9 Castle Street, until his own early death in January 1872. A contemporary description in the Packer scrapbook gives some idea of the solemnity and grandeur of a Victorian funeral in Ludlow. It begins with the letter to Robert's widow from the Ludlow Board of Guardians, for whom he acted as Clerk:

Dear Madam,

At a meeting of the Ludlow Board of Guardians held January 17th 1872, it was unanimously resolved to offer to you, and to the rest of Mr Lloyd's family, the expression of their heartfelt regret at his decease, and that I as their chairman should be desired to convey this to you.

During the ten years of Mr Lloyd's clerkship to this Union, he has given constant proofs of his high ability, of his close attention to his duties, and of his unselfish readiness to carry out the wishes of the Board without regard to his own trouble.

The guardians feel conscious that they have been unusually fortunate in having thus obtained the services of a gentleman who, while giving a minute attention to the smallest details in the routine of his office, was able to take a wider view of the interests it involved. They are aware of the advantages they have derived from his legal knowledge and at the same time they have had reason to appreciate his extensive and kindly acquaintance with the Union and its inhabitants. Their regret corresponds with their loss. Your loss, however, far exceeds that of any other of Mr Lloyd's friends, and instead of intruding upon you at any length at such a moment, I shall best carry out the wishes of the Board by assuring you of their sincere sympathy with you in your bereavement.

I am, Dear Madam, yours faithfully,
George J. Corser
Chairman of the Ludlow Board of Guardians

The entry continues with an account of the funeral:

We last week noticed the death of Mr Lloyd, and to which we may now add that the funeral obsequies afforded an opportunity for indicating the very general regret throughout the town. With very few exceptions the whole of the shops were partially closed. Three mourning coaches conveyed R. Lightbody, F. R.E. Lloyd, Leominster; E. Mott, London; F. R. Southern, H. Hodges, J. Tench, R. Tench, G. Hodges, and C.Peele, Shrewsbury, Esqrs., the Rector of Ludlow, and the Rev. Meyricke, and the medical attendants. Following the coaches there were the clerks of the firm of Southern and Lloyd, the Master and Officers of the Union Workhouse and the undertakers. The deceased having been a member of the church choir, the 39th Psalm was chanted and the 191st hymn was sung by the choir of St Leonard's Chapel. The coffin bore the inscription: 'Robert William Lloyd, born August 1832, died January 1872.

On Sunday evening in the church of St Laurence, a funeral hymn was sung, and the 'Dead March in Saul' was effectively given on the organ by Mr Bartholomew at the close of the service.

No women, of course, were in the procession, nor at the service. It may be that Fanny, John's widow, already struck down by the death of her eldest son, John Charles, the previous November, was unable to go, but at this time, women did not usually attend funerals, though they went into mourning for many months.

The thirteen-year-old Princess Victoria and her mother had visited Ludlow on 4th November 1832 on their way from Oakly Park, as she made one of her tours of the country, but the town's great days as a fashionable social centre had passed. Nevertheless there continued to be many changes in Ludlow throughout the nineteenth century. The 'tumbledown' rooms in the market house had been superseded by fine new assembly rooms designed by Matthew Stead & Son in 1838. The three Lloyd brothers, John, William and Thomas, were among the shareholders, and William and Thomas were on the committee set up to manage and superintend the affairs of the company which was to buy the land and erect the building. Dr Lloyd took the chair. Assemblies were to take place every fortnight from October to March, open to anyone who could afford a ticket, though when the American visitor, Anna Maria Fay, attended a ball in January 1851, she found 'none but ladies and gentlemen there'. She thought it curious to see 'a Public Ball so select'.[136]

Transport had steadily improved since the Lybbe Powyses had jolted along the turnpike roads of Shropshire, well-known as a place of 'bad roads and long journeys'.[137] In the early eighteenth century, it took seven days to get to London, but by 1794 there were four coaches a week between Ludlow and the metropolis and the fastest took only twenty-four hours. By 1811 things had improved still further. There were good carrier services to take goods by wagon and cart, and nearly twenty passenger and mail coaches to and from London every week via Worcester or Oxford; by 1844 there were forty coaches a week. From the Crown and the Angel regular services ran to Shrewsbury, Hereford and Bristol and into Wales.[138] As Thomas Johnes of Hafod wrote to a friend in 1796, 'you will be surprised when I tell you there are two diligences, as I hear, coming to the Devil's Bridge and Aberystwyth from Leominster and Ludlow by different roads'. In 1805 he commented, 'A mail coach runs once a week from Ludlow … I never remember so many *curious* travellers as this year'.[139] Some of the coaches had splendid names such as the Prince Regent Coach and the Defiance, and it must have been exciting to rattle under the arch and out into the countryside, or to hear the guard's post-horn signalling the arrival of the Hereford coach as it came up the street and approached the Broad Gate (see Fig. 40). But it still took thirty-one hours to travel from Ludlow to London by the slow coach, and six hours to Shrewsbury. Even at a smart trot, Henry Lloyd would have needed two or three hours to ride on horseback to Weobley to oversee Lord Bath's estates and to keep an eye on his cattle.

Anna Maria Fay had come from Boston for a year to visit her American relatives, who were renting Moor Park from the Salweys. Her stay coincided with the coming of the railway to Ludlow on April 20th 1852. She wrote back to her family, describing the reception for the first train and the town's celebrations, including the erection of arches of greenery over the streets and on the fronts of the inns. There was a huge press of people, and a déjeuner held by the contractor, Mr Brassey, for three hundred selected guests. Other events were held during the day for everyone to mark the occasion – sports at the Castle, clowns and stilt-walkers in the streets – and a ball in the evening, which was, in theory, open to everyone.[140] This was one of the balls for which Lady Trimelstown (whom Anna Maria calls 'Lady Trembleson') was a patron. In May, Anna Maria and her relatives went by train to the races at Shrewsbury:

47. THE ANGEL INN, LUDLOW
This mail coach ran from the 1790s and reached London in twenty-four hours. Thomas Bowen,
one of James Kinnersley's former servants, leased the Angel in 1794, and by 1800 the owner
was Elizabeth Toldervy, Samuel Sprott's niece

> *We left Ludlow in the train at quarter past ten, and arrived at*
> *Shrewsbury at quarter after twelve, thus making the distance of*
> *twenty-seven miles in two hours, but when you know that there are*
> *ten stations on the way, it is not so very long ... We arrived home*
> *about half-past eight o'clock ... the journey over and back costing us*
> *five shillings and sixpence, the fare only one way every day.*[141]

As Mrs Lybbe Powys had already noted in 1771, spas and seaside towns were proving ever more attractive to visitors, and, although, with the improvement of the roads and the coming of the railways, people could reach the town more easily, Ludlow's inhabitants could also leave more easily for larger and more exciting destinations. When Henry James visited the town in the 1870s he found it:

> *a ruin – the most impressive and magnificent of ruins. The charming old town and the admirable castle form a capital object of pilgrimage. Ludlow is an excellent example of a small English provincial town that has not been soiled and disfigured by industry; it exhibits no tall chimneys and smoke-streamers, with their attendant purlieus and slums. The little city is perched upon a hill near which the goodly Severn [actually the Teme] wanders, and it has a remarkable air of civic dignity. Its streets are wide and clean, empty and a little grass-grown, and bordered with spacious, mildly-ornamental brick houses, which look as if there had been more going on in them in the first decade of the century than there is in the present, but which can still hold up their heads and keep their window-panes clear, their knockers brilliant and their door steps whitened. The place seems to say that a hundred years, and less, ago it was the centre of a large provincial society, and that this society was very 'good' of its kind. It must have transported itself to Ludlow for the season in rumbling coaches and heavy curricles – and there entertained itself in decent emulation of that metropolis which a choice of railway lines had not as yet placed within its immediate reach … It is a place on which a provincial 'gentry' has left a sensible stamp. I have seldom seen so good a collection of houses of the period between the elder picturesqueness and the modern baldness … a genteel little city like the one I am speaking of must have been a kind of focus of insular propriety.*[142]

By this time, however, the Victorians had become more interested in the romantic view of the medieval past of the town than in its Georgian phase. This is well illustrated by Evans's *Guidebook to Ludlow* of 1860:

*… the only remaining gateway [is] Broad Gate. This alone has
withstood the ravages of time, and the still more ruthless hand of
the barbarous leveller of all antiquities which has no respect for the
skill, the valour and perseverance of our noble ancestors, who were
driven to extremities in protection of their families … thus the Broad
Gate is of peculiar interest. Here are still to be seen the hinges upon
which sat the inner gate of safety, the very groove down which sliced
the ponderous portcullis, the sentinel's box, the whispering crevice
through which the messages were sent to the town authorities, and
even the hook upon which hung the horse's bridle of the messenger
while awaiting commands. Outside was the drawbridge over the
moat, afterwards a stone bridge, the arches of which remain.*

The difference between eighteenth-century Gothick and Victorian Gothic
Revival is as much one of attitude as appearance. At Strawberry Hill Horace
Walpole had exact copies made of features from medieval buildings, but
his house bears little resemblance to an actual medieval castle or church,
and is more of a jeu d'esprit. Like Shobdon Church or the Broad Gate house
and chambers, it is a playful fantasy. Eighteenth century Gothick, it has
been said, was 'a decorator's style, frivolous, light-hearted, improbable and
escapist'.[143] In contrast, the Victorians were deadly serious in their intention
to impose their version of the medieval on to domestic architecture as well
as churches, and, in churches in particular, they destroyed many genuine
medieval and Georgian interiors. In Ludlow this movement took the form
of removing the render from timber-framed buildings, stripping undressed
stone and brutally 'restoring' the church.

The town and the country were still very interdependent. Younger sons
of the gentry and members of yeoman families were increasingly going into
the urban professions, so that the line between the gentry and the middling
sort was becoming blurred. In any case, many upper-class families had

made their original fortunes from commerce, law and other professions. Lawyers, in particular, like the Lloyds at the Broad Gate, could become very prosperous. There were also plenty of people who retired to Ludlow from elsewhere, bringing their wealth with them. They found Ludlow an attractive and congenial place to live – as many still do today. The inhabitants of the town took full advantage of the pleasures of the river, the woods and the countryside around. The Boating Club was restricted to the middle classes, but river sports and skating in the winter were enjoyed by all ranks, and everyone could ramble in the woods or over Whitcliffe, or go to the races. The common land protected the town from the south and west, but to the north and east, outside its walls, the suburbs grew; first the Teme and the Corve and then the railway were the boundaries.

The social prestige may have gone, and the glove industry, on which Ludlow had depended for many years and which had supported several hundred people, men, women and children, was declining as a result of competition from abroad. Malting and brewing, paper and cloth-making were also hit by the improvement in transport from larger centres. Nevertheless, the town, with its crucial live-stock markets, survived the agricultural depression better than towns in arable areas. There was an expansion in dealers, and it was a bustling centre for the local farmers and their wives. With its food markets and other shops, its lawyers and doctors, it was still a meeting place for the countryside around. Moreover, between Ludlow and its hinterland, the connections were not just social, but increasingly financial and political. In the eighteenth century, and well into the nineteenth, the Herbert and Clive families treated Ludlow as a pocket borough, dominating the Corporation until 1835 and returning members of Parliament. Edward Herbert, Lord Clive, held one of the two parliamentary seats from 1806 to 1839. Nothing changed for many years, but the families' influence was fading. There were fewer gentry members of the Corporation, and tradesmen and manufacturers came to play a larger

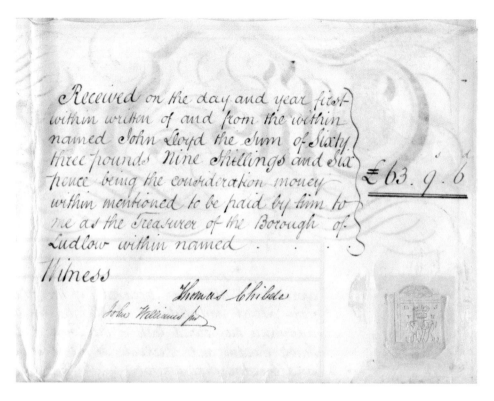

48. PART OF A LEGAL DOCUMENT FROM 1852
which conveyed the freehold of the Broad Gate to John Lloyd

part in governing the town – as they had done before 1700, especially once the ratepayers began electing the new Borough Councils. A major crisis arose over St Leonard's Chapel, a medieval building with a burial ground at the bottom of Corve Street, the care of which had become the responsibility of the Corporation in 1771. After years of neglect, the chapel had been dismantled to provide stone for the repair of Corve Bridge. Henry Lloyd had himself headed a committee set up by St Laurence's in 1814 to establish the ownership of the chapel, and in the following year a case was brought against the Corporation in the Court of Chancery. They were ordered to build a new chapel, which they finally did in 1870.[144]

The most contentious issue, though, which became known as 'The Great Law Case', arose over the Corporation's administration of the Palmers' Guild Charities and the land and property that funded them. These had been handed over to the Corporation in 1551, but the proportion of the revenue passed on to the Charities had diminished over the years, with the Council keeping most of it. A compromise was reached, but the Clives, anxious to keep in with the town, opposed it. Among the Charities, the almshouses were championed by Edmund Lechmere Charlton, who had a grudge against the Clives, and the Grammar School by the Rev. Arthur Willis, its Headmaster, who had ambitions to expand the school. The dispute became extremely acrimonious and went to the Court of Chancery, where in 1845 the Lord Chancellor found for the Charities. Their income was increased and costs were awarded against the Corporation, which had by this time become an elected Borough Council under the Municipal Corporation Act of 1835.[145]

The enormous sum due meant that the Council had to sell off its property in the town. At one time the Palmers' Guild and then the Corporation had owned a third of all the town's buildings, and Council property was still a large estate. Most of it was now sold to existing lease-holders, thereby enabling John Lloyd to buy the freehold of the Broad Gate in 1852 for £63. 9s. 6d, a bargain. He continued to pay a ground rent, but he now owned the freehold of one of the most important residences in the town.

49. *THE COPPER BEECH ON THE EDGE OF THE TOWN WALL*
probably planted in 1814. The grafting mark is still apparent

– 10 –

THE LATER LLOYDS

During the Victorian period, the Lloyds made comparatively few changes to the house itself. An attempt was made to bring the dining-room up to date by inserting a larger grey marble fireplace in the place of the eighteenth century original, though its design mirrored that of the older stone fireplace in the hall. There was also an ingenious solution to the problem of a square dining-room with doors, windows or fireplace in each wall, allowing no space for a sideboard. A mahogany folding table was inserted across one corner with a hinged flap which could be let down as a serving-table. There are one or two other examples of this unusual arrangement in Ludlow. In the drawing-room, the long windows facing the garden were replaced with plate glass, and on each side of the arch connecting the two parlours, carved *cartouches* with shields were placed, no doubt to carry coats of arms. At some stage, a cast iron verandah was built against the garden front, though this had disappeared by the beginning of the twentieth century. Three generations of Lloyd children had the long garden to play in, as well as the Lower Garden in the town ditch, where there was later a tennis court.

Inside there would have been major changes in the disposition of the furniture to create an even more informal and sociable atmosphere. The catalogue of the final sale of the contents of the house in 1940 shows what a

50. AN EARLY PRINT OF 1825
showing the two horse chestnut trees already well-established

huge amount of Victorian furniture had been added to the Georgian items inherited by the family. From the time of William IV, furniture had become heavier and more ornate. As the Victorian age continued, there would have been far more knicknacks and whatnots, and probably darker or more elaborate decoration. One surround to the open shelves in the west bedroom has revealed on the back some florid flock wallpaper. No doubt there were also improvements in the kitchen and laundry areas, though the Aga arrived only in the 1960s or 70s. On the whole, however, very little changed during the long period of Fanny Lloyd's widowhood, from 1869 to 1915. The top room of the new chambers, though always called 'the library', had become the family sitting-room by 1920, when Edward Stanley, his wife and three children moved in, leaving the drawing room as a more formal reception room for visitors. As Humphry Repton wrote as early as 1816, 'The most recent modern custom is to use the library as the general family living-room;

51. AN EARLY PHOTOGRAPHIC VIEW SHOWING THE TALLER OF THE TREES
taken from Lower Broad Street in 1865

and that sort of state room formerly called the best parlour, and of late years the drawing room, is now found a melancholy apartment, when entirely shut up and opened to give visitors a formal cold reception'.[146] In many houses, well into the twentieth century, this was the frigid 'front room'.

Throughout the nineteenth century the exterior view of the house from Broad Street changed considerably with the planting of two horse chestnut trees by the front door where there now stands a clipped yew. These appear, already quite mature, in a print of Broad Street in the 1820s. One grew to an

52. A VIEW FROM THE BROAD GATE UP BROAD STREET,
showing the steps and palisade at the side, and one of the chestnut trees, in about 1812,
possibly painted by William Gwynne, 1782-c.1860

immense height; it reached well above the roof of the house and can be seen in many views taken from Lower Broad Street, beginning with the Ziegler watercolour of 1825, and continuing in scores of photographs. It was finally cut down in 1922, but another tree, planted early in the century, a copper beech on the edge of the town wall, still dominates the garden. This tree has been judged to be anything from one hundred and fifty to two hundred and fifty years old, but it is likely that it was planted in 1814 to celebrate what was thought, wrongly, to be the final defeat of Napoleon. With its great girth and grafting mark it is similar in circumference to those at Fonmon Castle in the Vale of Glamorgan, which are known to have been planted at that time and for that reason. Another change to the view of the house was the demolition of the steps into Silk Mill Lane from the terrace outside numbers 35, 36 and 37 on the western side of Broad Street. This terrace had been built in 1757, when the Corporation gave permission to Thomas Dunne 'to raise up before his freehold house (35 and 36) a terrace walk as high as his outward doorstep, with railings and palisades to be used as a common footpath'. A wooden chinoiserie palisade with steps leading down to Silk Mill Lane is shown in a watercolour of about 1812, which also shows one of the trees. Around 1858, a descendant, Thomas Dunne of Gatley Park, was given the Corporation's permission to remove the steps, giving himself and his neighbour, Miss Rogers at No. 37, more privacy.[147]

John Lloyd's first wife, Charlotte Hodges, died in 1854 leaving no children. Two years later, on 17th April 1856, he married Frances Maria Pinhorn (Fanny). She was twenty-five at the time and he was fifty-nine. She was the daughter of the Rev. George Pinhorn of Rock in Worcestershire who had retired to Brimfield. According to the *Eddowes Journal and General Advertiser* for 23rd April:

> *The public, anxious to behold the bridal party, assembled in large numbers in the street from Mr Lloyd's house to the … parish church of St Laurence's. The cortège [sic] consisted of various carriages containing a fine array of female beauty. During the day, the fine old bells of St Laurence's church sent forth their merry peals.*

John and Fanny had seven children in thirteen years, and when he died in 1869 she remained a widow at the Broad Gate for a further forty-six years. Their first children were Fanny Louisa (Louie) born in March 1857 and John Charles born in 1858. There followed in roughly two-year intervals three more daughters and two more sons. John Charles, the eldest son, may have been born a sickly child or became ill later, because when he died of scarlet fever in 1871, aged thirteen, the property that he would have inherited after the death of his father in 1869, was already vested in his younger brother,

George Frederick, perhaps because it was clear that he was not going to be able to inherit the estate.

The remaining two sons became professional men. George Frederick, born in 1866, was a clergyman, but died aged thirty-three in 1897. With his and John's early deaths, Edward Stanley, (known as Stanley) born in 1868, despite being the youngest child, became the senior Lloyd. He had spent at least a year at Shrewsbury School when he was about fifteen, but he left to follow the family tradition and became a solicitor in the firm of Southern, Lloyd and Appleton, based in Ludlow, no longer at the Broad Gate chambers, but at 9 Castle Square. In the course of his career, he was commissioner for oaths, clerk to the governors of the Girls' High School, agent for the Alliance Fire and Life insurance company and a magistrate. In 1900, he married in London Amy Louisa Lewis, the daughter of a Montgomery clergyman, David Lewis, who had come to live in Ludlow.[148] She was the great-niece of Nerry Lewis, Henry Lloyd's second wife. In the *Shrewsbury Chronicle* she is described as 'the younger daughter of the late Rev. D. Phillips, Rector of Llandrinio and Rural Dean, and sister of Colonel Lewis CB, who has won honour and fame by his excellent service in the Sudan'. Stanley and Amy lived outside Ludlow, at Whitton, with their three children until 1920, four years after Fanny's death, when they moved into the Broad Gate.

Stanley's sister, Ethel Mary ('Effie') remained a spinster and lived with her mother. Alice, who was nearest to him in age, married Francis Southern, a relative of the earlier Francis Southern who had married William Lloyd's daughter, Fanny, and a partner in the Lloyd practice. The two remaining sisters both married clergymen: Louie married the Rev. Alfred Wight in 1885; Annie married the Rev. Geoffrey Wyatt Turner in November 1895. He had been lecturer at St Laurence's for fifteen years, but had just been appointed to the living of Madley in Herefordshire. The *Wellington Journal and Shrewsbury Times* (which appears to have been Fanny's favourite paper) reported the wedding:

*The bridegroom, accompanied by his best man, the Rev. L. C.
Wilkinson, entered the church some time before the ceremony. The
bride, who was attired in a dress of ivory brocade silk, with wreath
and veil, and carrying a lovely bouquet of white flowers, entered
the church leaning on the arm of her eldest brother, the Rev. George
Lloyd. The bridesmaids were Miss Lloyd (sister of the bride) and Miss
Turner (sister of the bridegroom) who wore dresses of salmon pink silk
trimmed with white silk, with hats to match, and carried bouquets of
dark flowers. The first part of the ceremony was performed by the Rev.
J. R. Turner, rector of Wroughton, Wiltshire, father of the bridegroom.
The Psalm was chanted by the choir. The second part was performed
by the Rev. Prebendary Clayton, rector of Ludlow. The anthem was
'Lord, for Thy tender mercies' sake' and hymn 210, 'Gracious Spirit,
Holy Ghost', was sung by the choir. As the party entered the church a
soft voluntary was played on the organ by Mr J. Atkins, organist, and
as they left the altar, the Wedding March (Lohengrin) was performed
… On leaving the church, rice was showered upon them.*

As at John and Fanny's wedding thirty years before, 'the bells of St
Laurence rang out merry peals'.

The happy couple left by the 4.36 train for the honeymoon.

It was usual at the time for the description of the ceremony to be followed
by an even longer list of the wedding presents and their donors. The couple
received a great deal of silver, some cheques, a 'Chippendale' mirror and
tea-table, a breakfast service and a crumb tray among many other household
items, including a framed picture of Ludlow Castle. The Broad Gate servants
gave a lamp.

A photograph of some of her Pinhorn relatives outside the drawing-room
window was probably taken in 1914 on the occasion of Fanny's eighty-fifth
birthday. When she died in 1915, the family's property consisted of the Broad

53. FANNY LLOYD SURROUNDED BY HER PINHORN RELATIVES
possibly on the occasion of her eighty-fifth birthday in 1914
(back row, from left) Louie Wight, daughter; Amy Lloyd, daughter-in-law; Florence Gill, sister;
Stanley, son; Alda Brown, sister; Alda Brown, niece; Rosamond Gill, niece;
Lawrence Gill, nephew; Cecil Wight, grandson; (front row, from left) Effie Lloyd, daughter;
Evan Lloyd, grandson; Fanny Lloyd; George Lloyd, grandson; James Wight, grandson

Gate itself, with its legal chambers, land in the town ditch and the gardener's cottage in Silk Mill Lane, together with the house, yard and premises of St Leonard's House on the corner of the churchyard, of which the family now owned the freehold. At this time it was let on a yearly tenancy, with the stable nearby, where the Upper Linney meets College Street, which was also let, on a quarterly tenancy. Apart from a bequest to her gardener, William Bayfield, Fanny left her personal estate equally between her five remaining children, Stanley, Louie, Effie, Annie and Alice, with an extra £1,000 to Effie, who had never married. After her mother's death, she moved to a flat at 9 Castle Street, where her brother practised as a solicitor, and where she lived until her own death twenty years later. This was the building once owned by Isabella Sprott, Samuel Sprott's spinster aunt, from 1727 to 1733.

There were problems attached to the Broad Gate itself. Although John Lloyd, as a solicitor, should have known better, he had died intestate in 1869. His eldest son, John Charles, died two years later in 1871 as a minor, also intestate. George Frederick, the next brother, had succeeded legally to the title in 1871, before John Charles's death, but he too died young in 1897, aged thirty-one, again intestate. At that date, Fanny renounced the letters of administration for the property, which were granted to Stanley. But after her death, he had to prove the capacity of John Charles, and his own right to succeed. He had letters of administration which gave him the right to live at the Broad Gate, where he and his family moved in 1920, but it was not until 1926 that the estate was finally vested in him.[149] Stanley and his family lived at the Broad Gate for twenty years, until 1940.

When the First World War broke out, Stanley had fortunately been too old to fight and his sons too young. But his first son, Evan John Stanley, who was born in 1902 and had been to Clifton College, attended the Royal Military Academy at Woolwich and passed out as a second lieutenant on 31st August 1922. He was commissioned into the Royal Artillery, but died young in an accident at Larkhill, Salisbury, the artillery training site, in 1924.

The second son, George Hallowes Lloyd, was born in 1903. He also attended Clifton College. His middle name was the maiden name of his maternal grandmother, Louisa Lewis née Hallowes. Her family came from Derbyshire and was distinguished in many fields, particularly in the armed services. They had aristocratic connections and, like the Lloyds, traced their origins back to royalty, in fact quite convincingly to Edward III. Louisa

54. THE LLOYD FAMILY IN THE BROAD GATE GARDEN AROUND 1920
From left to right: Stanley, Mary, George, Amy, Evan and Dick, the dog

Hallowes had married the Rev. David Lewis, son of the Dr David Lewis who is commemorated in the Lady Chapel of St. Laurence's. Dr Lewis, who died in 1837, was the son of John Lewis, a joiner, and his wife Elizabeth, who lived at 50 Broad Street. He served in the Bengal Medical Service before returning to live in Worcester. He married his cousin, Caroline, who was living at 54 Broad Street in 1841, and he was the brother of Henry Lloyd's second wife, Anne Harriet Lewis ('Nerry'). Her great-niece, Louisa Lewis, the mother of Stanley's wife, Amy Louisa, was living at the Broad Gate after the

55. GEORGE HALLOWES LLOYD, 1903-1986

death of Fanny Lloyd in 1915 and died there in August 1918. Her widowed daughter, Caroline (Mrs Egerton), George's aunt, was also living at the house in 1917.

After leaving school, George Lloyd tried fruit farming in British Columbia, and worked for a rubber company in Malaya, but returned to England in 1933. When the Second World War began, he enlisted as a 2nd lieutenant in the 1st Herefordshire Regiment. He served with this regiment throughout the war, becoming a Captain in March 1942. He was in France and northern Europe from June 1944 until the end of the war.

The third child, Mary Louisa, was born at Whitton on 14th March 1909. She had the rare distinction of having a grandfather born in the eighteenth century. She moved to the Broad Gate with her family at the age of eleven and

*56. MARY LOUISA LLOYD, 1909-1994
wearing her great-grandmother's ring*

spent most of her early life there. As the youngest child and only girl, she always felt overshadowed by her brothers, and resented the fact that, at the age of eight, she was sent away to boarding school, while they, at the time, were still at home. Her mother died in 1932. Like her brothers, Mary never married. She was apparently courted at one time, but her parents did not approve of the young man and she was sent off on a world tour to forget him. Possibly under the influence of the precious law library built up by her great-grandfather, Henry, which she kept, she later became interested in antiquarian books and added to the collection from the bookshops in Ludlow. She was also very fond of jewellery, and inherited her great-grandmother, Thomasin's, ring. In 1940 when her father and her aunt both died, she moved to a country cottage at Yatton, in Herefordshire, and in the 1950s was living at Ladyridge Farm, Brockhampton.

After he returned from the army, George never worked again. For a while he lived at Ringwood in Hampshire, but then built himself a house at Woolhope in Herefordshire. Later he moved with his sister Mary to a cottage at Fownhope, where he made a beautiful garden. He was something of a recluse and may have suffered from his experiences during the war, but there was still plenty of money in the family and they had been well provided for, so he and Mary were able to live on private means. When their father and their aunt both died in 1940, the Broad Gate had been left to George and Mary jointly, but it seems that Mary was responsible for disposing of the house. She had no alternative but to sell it.

Just as in 1813, this was a bad time to sell a house, particularly such an unusual house. It was put up for sale on March 27th 1940 by John Norton, the Ludlow auctioneers, but once again it failed to find a buyer. The sale notice described the house as a 'Historical Residence', with its grounds of 3 Roods and 28 Perches. In the eighteenth century Samuel Sprott had acquired extra land to the south of the town ditch in Lower Broad Street which had been bought from Samuel Yate Sprott by the Kinnersleys. The Lloyds had also bought property in the town, and still owned 73 and 74 Lower Broad Street, which were included in the sale.

In early April this unsuccessful auction was followed by a 'highly important and interesting' three-day sale of the contents of the house. Although there had been earlier sales of books and furniture after Fanny's death, the auction included furniture, paintings, books, china and a vast accumulation of household objects acquired over a hundred and twenty-four years and possibly longer. The main attraction, printed in red, was 'Early English Furniture of the 17th and 18th Centuries, viz. Important Chippendale and other Georgian period Glazed Escritoire bookcases in Mahogany'. Other highlights included Persian rugs; oriental and English carpets; about 300 ozs. of Georgian and other silver; old Sheffield plate; antique English, oriental and continental porcelain and pottery; 1,000 volumes of books; and 'Costly Modern Furnishings'. Everything else on the premises was for sale. The catalogue begins with the silver and china and ends with a quantity of wire pea guards and an iron pig trough. With some late additions, there were 746 lots. This time, in spite of the depressed market, the sale was quite successful.

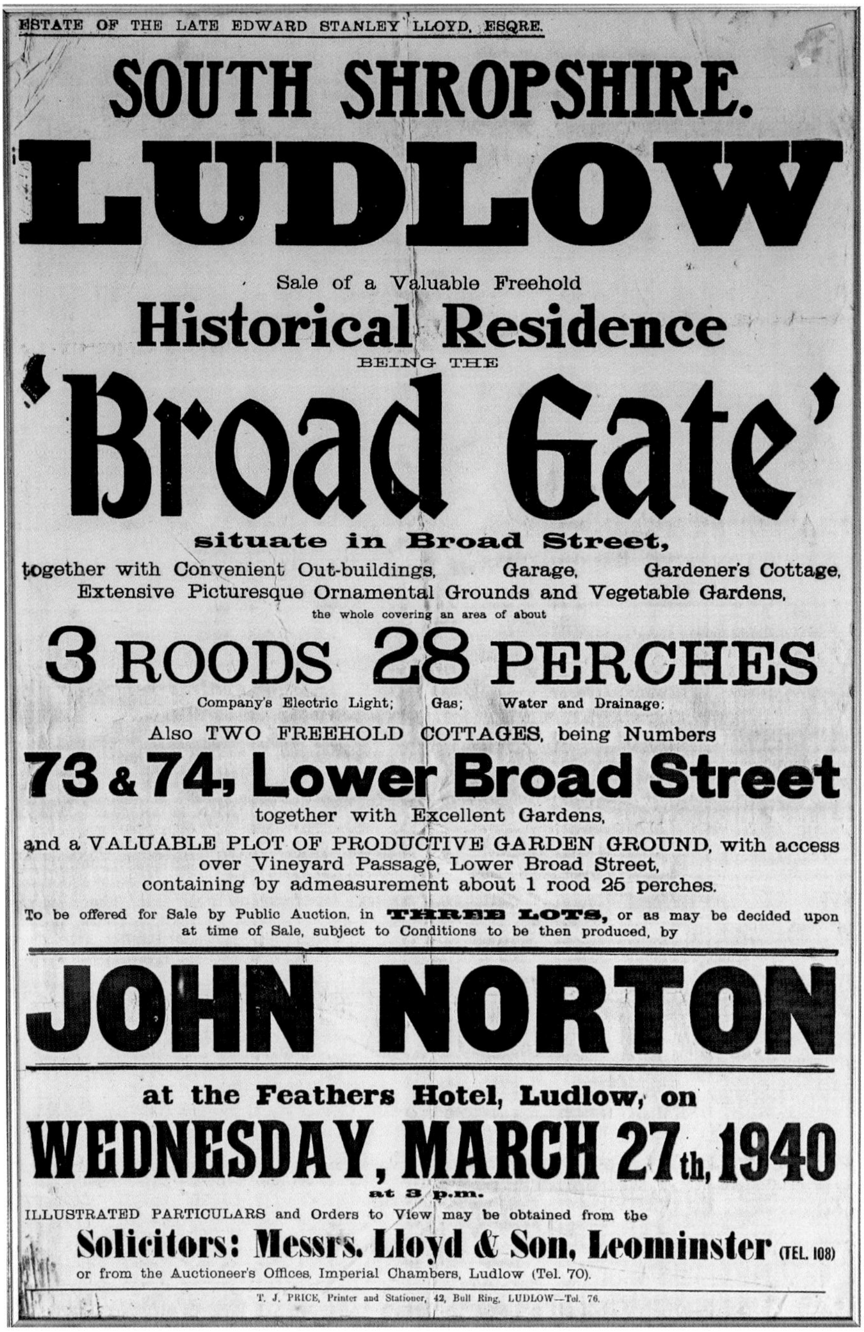

ESTATE OF THE LATE EDWARD STANLEY LLOYD, ESQRE.

SOUTH SHROPSHIRE.

LUDLOW

Sale of a Valuable Freehold

Historical Residence

BEING THE

'Broad Gate'

situate in Broad Street,

together with Convenient Out-buildings, Garage, Gardener's Cottage, Extensive Picturesque Ornamental Grounds and Vegetable Gardens,

the whole covering an area of about

3 ROODS 28 PERCHES

Company's Electric Light; Gas; Water and Drainage;

Also TWO FREEHOLD COTTAGES, being Numbers

73 & 74, Lower Broad Street

together with Excellent Gardens,

and a VALUABLE PLOT OF PRODUCTIVE GARDEN GROUND, with access over Vineyard Passage, Lower Broad Street, containing by admeasurement about 1 rood 25 perches.

To be offered for Sale by Public Auction, in THREE LOTS, or as may be decided upon at time of Sale, subject to Conditions to be then produced, by

JOHN NORTON

at the Feathers Hotel, Ludlow, on

WEDNESDAY, MARCH 27th, 1940

at 3 p.m.

ILLUSTRATED PARTICULARS and Orders to View may be obtained from the

Solicitors: Messrs. Lloyd & Son, Leominster (TEL. 108)

or from the Auctioneer's Offices, Imperial Chambers, Ludlow (Tel. 70).

T. J. PRICE, Printer and Stationer, 42, Bull Ring, LUDLOW—Tel. 76.

57. SALE NOTICE OF 1940, WHEN THE HOUSE REMAINED UNSOLD

Whether or not the furniture really was genuine Chippendale, Hepplewhite or Sheraton, some of the pieces sold very well. Lot 338, described as a six-foot long Chippendale mahogany pedestal writing table, possibly Henry's own desk, made £100, the equivalent of nearly £5,500 in today's money. A mahogany Chippendale escritoire with pierced cornice made half that amount, five Hepplewhite chairs were sold for £43 and a Sheraton serpentine inlaid satinwood chest of drawers for £30. A Chippendale walnut chinoiserie side table went for eleven guineas, and an early English bracket clock for eighteen guineas, the equivalent of about £1,000. A splendid Hepplewhite bedstead in the best bedroom, surmounted by a painted cornice

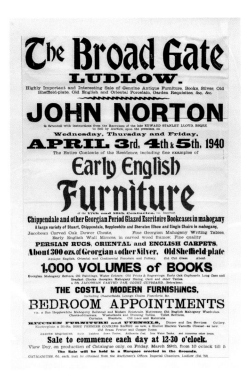

58. SALE NOTICE OF THE CONTENTS, FURNITURE AND EFFECTS
accumulated over three generations of the Lloyd family

in floral panels, which had fluted tapering pillars with tessellated and acanthus leaf carving, and its original Chinese-design hangings, made £12. A vast blue floral Staffordshire dinner service of eighty-one pieces went for £3.10s, but an even larger Worcester pink-rimmed dinner service of a hundred pieces made £8.10s.

George and Mary kept some family possessions, but they were sold after Mary's death in 1994. She left her books, including those which had belonged to her great-grandfather, to a cousin, who became an antiquarian bookseller as a result. Several of the family portraits found their way to relatives in America, but some were later returned to Mary's second cousin, Michael Lloyd. There are two eighteenth-century portraits of 'gentlemen' mentioned in the catalogue, one 'wearing a white cravat', which may well be a version of the portrait of Henry Lloyd, and a portrait of 'an elderly lady', but it is impossible to say whether any of them had any connection to the family. Some objects which suggest the life of the Lloyds in the nineteenth and early twentieth century, are tennis rackets, cricket bats and croquet sets, together with a collection of British birds' eggs in a specimen cabinet. Antlers also suggest, perhaps, an earlier connection with ancient country pursuits. There are boxes of toys and a 'large doll's house'; and the inclusion of a cottage piano in a walnut case by A. Bord of Paris suggests that someone in the household was musical. A number of Indian and Burmese objects are also what one would expect to find in a family of this era, perhaps the result of Dr Thomas Lloyd's three years in India. Apart from the furniture, silver and china, though, there are antique objects left over from previous centuries, such as a collection of old lace, an antique embroidered bedspread, antique silk shawls, two old enamel patch boxes, and a pair of antique swords with 'damascened' blades.

Collections of books generally tell something about their owners, but in this case there is nothing very different from the usual country-house library, save perhaps its less emphasis on dogs, though the family certainly kept them. So many books were sold in boxes that it is difficult to be sure, but there is little evidence of an individual taste. There were the usual sets of Victorian novels, Thackeray and Disraeli in particular, and the poetry of Cowper and Byron, together with Shakespeare. As might be expected, there were plenty of law books and works on history and topography, including Lewis's *Topographical Dictionary of England* of 1831. There were many boxes of children's books. Some members of the family were seriously interested in gardening, railways, horses and foxhunting; there were sets of encyclopaedias and, of course, Burke's *Landed Gentry* and Burke's *Commoners.* But there were one or two rarities as well. A folio copy of John Speed's *Atlas of Great Britain* (1676) sold well at £25, though an epitome of his *Theatre of the Empire of Great Britain* failed to sell. The sale also included a fifteenth-century Herefordshire manor roll, and, intriguingly, a collection of Elizabethan and other sealed documents, chiefly referring to Westbury, near Shrewsbury. Westbury was the parish of John Pryce and his wife, née Anne Sprott, who left her collection of documents to her nephew Samuel. It is tempting to imagine that these are some of the same papers, but the connection cannot be proved.

59. A CURRENT VIEW FROM LUDFORD BRIDGE
showing that the battlements, the tower on the legal chambers and the railings are missing

– 11 –

THE RICHARDSONS
1946-1991

In 1941 the empty house was taken over by the Army Pay Corps for the duration of the war. In spite of a framed notice still in existence, which requires the soldiers to respect the historic building, a considerable amount of superficial damage was caused during this occupation. The staircase suffered from the pounding of military feet, one of the bedroom chimney-pieces was damaged, the ice house in the kitchen cellar became a dumping place for bottles, and iron bars were put on the garden door and the windows of the dining room, which the Pay Corps turned into an office. It may have been at this period that the original eighteenth-century chimney-piece in the present drawing room disappeared. Outside, the main casualty was the removal of the elegant railings in front of the Gothick extension, which had been carefully designed to match the stonework over the windows. These railings, together with millions of others not considered necessary to edge areas or high walls, were commandeered to provide metal for the war effort, but many of them were never used and later dumped in the sea off Beachy Head. Correspondence survives from 1941-42 from the War Office, negotiating a rent for the backyard below the house,[150] but the town ditch and the garden itself appear to have been neglected for five or six years.

THIS BUILDING IS OF HISTORIC INTEREST & POSSESSES FEATURES OF ARCHITECTURAL IMPORTANCE. PANELLING, DOORS, CHIMNEY PIECES, ORNAMENTAL PLASTER WORK ETC. MUST NOT BE DAMAGED IN ANY WAY. NO ALTERATIONS OR REDECORATIONS ARE TO BE CARRIED OUT WITHOUT THE PRIOR CONSENT BOTH OF THE QUARTERING COMMANDANT & OF THE MINISTRY OF WORKS.

60. A NOTICE FROM THE MINISTRY OF WORKS
hanging in the house when it was occupied by the Pay Corps during the Second World War

61. THE HOUSE IN WARTIME,
when it was painted 'an indeterminate mud colour', and the barn next door, used by a builder,
was roofed with corrugated iron

After the war, as executors of their father's will, Mary and George put the Broad Gate up for sale again. On 5th December 1945 it was advertised in the *Birmingham Evening Post*, this time not as ' A Historical Residence', but as one in a list of properties to be auctioned:

Broad Gate House Ludlow. Freehold, early possession. Can be viewed any time.

It was bought in January 1946 by Mrs Annie Richardson, from Bishop's Castle, for £2,470. She had a husband, James, and two children, but she bought the house in her own name. Mrs Richardson now owned the whole of the main house with its extension, its back yard and the town ditch, the stables and gardener's cottage in Silk Mill Lane and a garden that stretched to Mill Street.

The army had been in residence for most of the war years, and the house, and particularly its surroundings, had been seriously neglected. It was six months before the Richardsons found their way to the end of the garden, which was a jungle. It must have been the romantic medieval character of the house that appealed to them. We don't know what the interior looked like when they moved in, but during their forty-five years in the Broad Gate all the beams, wainscotting and fireplace in the hall, the staircase and even the internal frames in the hall windows were painted black. There were some very large oil paintings and a huge piece of black oak furniture in the hall. This all gave a very dark, mysterious feeling to the house. Apparently Mrs Richardson's idea of redecoration was to add another coat of black paint. She made few alterations to the main house, but the missing drawing-room chimney-piece was now replaced by a mock-stone, mock-Tudor fireplace.

The house with all its land was plainly too large for a family of four with no live-in servants. The bottom room of the Gothick chambers was therefore let as a shop, first for electrical goods and later for antiques. The library in the top room, which had been the Lloyds' sitting room, now housed only a

62. THE PASSAGE AND STAIRS IN THE TIME OF THE RICHARDSONS

billiard table. Most of the other rooms on the top floor of the main house were unused. So the Richardsons set about selling off parts of the property, and turning what remained into a manageable family home.

In 1961, the house itself was divided. On 30th March, Harold and Phyllis Edwards, who ran the electrical shop in the lower room of the Gothick chambers, bought the three Gothick rooms looking down Lower Broad Street, together with the room in the west drum tower, joined to the line of small rooms above the archway, and the bedroom in the east drum tower above the Broad Gate kitchen. This created a flying freehold. It did not make for a very satisfactory layout, but at the time the bottom Gothick room was the shop and the idea was for the room above to be an office and store-room. The top Gothick room was to be the main living-room, and the kitchen was to be in the room behind it. With bedrooms above, this made sense as a two-storey flat. In the event, the kitchen was made at the rear of the first-floor room, but when Helen Williams, former High Mistress of St Paul's

63. THE PASSAGE AND STAIRS TODAY

Girls' School, bought the house in 1998, it had ceased to be a shop and she brought the kitchen down to the ground floor. This resulted in an extremely perpendicular house. The Broad Gate itself retained its kitchen and scullery in the eastern drum tower, together with the rest of the Georgian house, the upper garden, the town ditch below the wall and the back yard. The old legal chambers and rooms above were renamed 'The Gatehouse'.

The next sale, in June 1965, was to Mrs Richardson's sister, Mrs Margaret Walker, who for £200 bought enough land at the west end of the garden on which to build a house, 1, Silk Mill Lane. On the plans it seems that the Richardsons retained the glasshouses which had been there since the late eighteenth century. In 1983, however, more of the garden was sold to

64. THE NEW BUNGALOW IN THE 'LOWER GARDEN'
visible from the Broad Gate kitchen garden, with the gable end of the gardener's cottage

the new owner of the house, Mrs Penelope Cameron, and the glasshouses disappeared. Also in June 1965, Mrs Richardson sold the land in the town ditch, called by the Lloyds the 'Lower Garden', to Terence and Joyce Murray. They built a bungalow on the land and in 1968 sold it to relatives with the rest of the town ditch garden, which they had bought from the Richardsons. The lower garden is particularly attractive, bounded as it is by the south-facing town wall. Broadgate Cottage in Silk Mill Lane, where Fanny Lloyd's gardener had lived, was sold to Elizabeth and Walter Forrest in October 1975, with a covenant to protect the privacy of the Broad Gate garden. The separate properties have changed hands several times in the last few years. The Richardsons kept the stable itself, adjoining Broadgate Cottage, as it makes an excellent garden shed.

James Richardson had been a bank official at Barclays in Bishop's Castle, and when the family moved to Ludlow, he worked at the King Street branch.

65. THE GARDEN ENTRANCE TO THE STABLE

Annie Richardson, his wife, was a great supporter of St Laurence's, and of the annual Ludlow Festival. She is said to have had a pilot's licence and was a woman of great energy who did not seem to feel the cold, which was just as well, as the Broad Gate in those days was an extremely cold house. Many of the main rooms faced north and the hall over the arch had what amounted to an extra uninsulated wall under the floor. Apart from the open fire in the drawing room and the Aga in the kitchen, there were only three storage heaters in the whole house. In spite of weeping sometimes with the cold when cleaning and polishing in the unheated hall, Bella Collier served the Richardsons devotedly and stayed on after them, working at the house for nearly fifty years. She was the source of much of the information about this period in its history. Her family came originally from the Lake District, but had settled in Corvedale. Bella and her sister, when still quite young, went into service in the house of Major Benson at Aston Hall, where she was properly trained as a housemaid. The highlight in her young life was when the Prime Minister, Stanley Baldwin, came to lunch. She married Jack Collier, a native

Ludlovian, and moved into Ludlow. Eventually, they lived conveniently round the corner in Lower Raven Lane. Bella loved the Broad Gate and took great pride in her work. She had two daughters and several grandsons, one of whom became the professional opera singer, Andrew Morris.

Not long after Bella came to the house in the 1950s, part of the wall in Silk Mill Lane, most of which was a retaining wall for the garden, fell down and had to be replaced. Unfortunately, no effort was made to match the stone and the wall was rebuilt with rather unsuitable brick, which is only now beginning to weather. The render on the northern side of the house, still visible in early photographs, had been replaced with rough cast; at first it was painted a dark brown colour, but later a more suitable light battleship grey, not perhaps an authentic Georgian shade, but praised by Alec Clifton-Taylor in his television series, 'Six English Towns' (August 1978). In April 1954 the house was listed as Grade 1, not so much for its interior, but because it is such an important focal point in Broad Street, closing the street at the south end, as the Buttercross does at the north. The town wall and the medieval part of the gate were designated an Ancient Monument in 1955.

Meanwhile, George and Mary Lloyd were still living in Herefordshire. He died in 1986 and she lived on until 1994. She supplied a good deal of information to Michael Lloyd, her second cousin (1928-2006), who was writing a history of the family, and she corresponded with the local historian, David Lloyd (no relation), who was studying the Broad Street houses. Two surviving letters that she wrote to him in 1976 give some idea of how the Lloyds used the house. She says, for instance, that the Lloyd family used the library at the top of the Gothick building as their sitting room, entered from the main house, and that in their day it was not directly connected with the rooms below. Describing a visit she made with a friend to the separated Gatehouse, she says:

They have cut another flight of stairs up into the top room where we used to sit always.

She had used the middle room of the three as her private sitting room, so there may have been some connecting staircase from the backstairs in the main house at that time. Her own bedroom was the room with the single window over the arch. Next to it, the room at the top of the eastern drum tower was a bathroom. 'It was a huge room, which had a bath in the corner and a basin and hot water tank and a cupboard, and stands in fact, immediately above the kitchen.' The water was connected by a pipe that ran through all of the bedrooms facing north, which had plumbed-in washstands. The waste water ran along the front of the house in an internal gutter behind the raised centre of the battlements, together with all the run-off water from the north-facing roof of the house, an arrangement which a modern surveyor regarded with horror, but which still works perfectly well. She also remarks on the arrow-slits, which had since the Lloyds' time been uncovered, and a window in the 'bathroom' in the eastern drum tower which is sometimes visible in photographs and sometimes not. Mary suggests that the new owner of the Gatehouse had 'opened an old window that must have been blocked in for hundreds of years'. In fact, according to Bella, it was at one time at the back of a cupboard and was therefore not needed, but was later reinstated. At some point, the thick eastern wall of that room in the drum tower was replaced with a thinner brick wall which gave an extra three feet to the room and allowed a projection from the tower to give another window to the south. This could have happened as early as the fire in 1700, but it is not present in the Ziegler print of 1826. Mary was surprised to see that in this room, the 'bathroom', where all the fittings had been removed, there was 'some very handsome half-timbering ... a beautiful internal gable end!'

Mary Lloyd also comments on the external appearance of the north front. 'The front of the house is flat all across and rough cast and has recently been done in a pale grey, which I think an improvement, as it was a sort of indeterminate mud colour before which made it look very dark indeed.' Within the house, she describes how someone came once to fix up a gas

66. *A PHOTOGRAPH TAKEN FROM LOWER BROAD STREET AROUND 1890*
showing the battlemented extension to the west of the legal chambers

fire in the convex tower wall at the back of the middle room of the Gothick chambers:

> *It took him nearly a whole day to get through the centre of the round [tower] – it is 7 ft thick!*

She refers, too, to the dungeon in the east tower, which she says had a door leading from the cellar under Chandler's Cottage, next to the arch, which must have been bricked up in 1945 by 'Mr Bryant,' who was, presumably, living there. The Richardsons confirmed her recollection.

Mary's most interesting observation concerns the two-storey extension to the west of the building. 'The bottom room of all was just a junk room full of extra furniture, and the clients ascended according to their importance... there was a little clutch of rooms built up against the outside of the main building, opening into the yard there, which I remember hearing of as clerks' offices.' She suggests that 'perhaps it was a little hideaway from Henry'. These rooms were accessed from the ground floor, but there was also an entrance from the middle room, the door case of which is still visible from inside. When this extension was demolished is not at all clear. The top was castellated to match the rest of the building; this is still visible in some twentieth-century photographs and in a couple of paintings, one dated 1930. Mary Lloyd would have known if it had been demolished while she was still living at the Broad Gate, so it is most likely that it vanished soon after the war, perhaps as part of the scheme in 1961 to divide the house, when a garage was put in its place.[151]

The Richardson children, Helen and John, grew up in the house and enjoyed exploring it. They were happy to play in the attics, but they thought the cellars too dark and creepy. John later moved abroad to work, and Helen married and moved to Birmingham. Their father died and their mother developed dementia, so, after forty-five years, the house was put up for sale again.

When Keith and Valerie Thomas bought the house in 1991, they, unlike their predecessors, were mainly concerned to restore the Georgian character of the interior. This was not difficult, as most of the changes in the intervening years had been cosmetic; it was a simple matter of knocking through bricked-up fireplaces to reveal the original Coalbrookdale grates, and repainting the rooms in paler Georgian colours. They also stripped the wallpaper from the kitchen, revealing the three small fire-boxes in the walls, restored the glazing bars to the long drawing-room windows, and replaced the drawing-

67. THE DRAWING ROOM CHIMNEY-PIECE
designed by Thomas Farnolls Pritchard,
originally for Broseley Hall

room fireplace with an original Pritchard rococo chimneypiece, documented in his notebook, from Broseley Hall. Apart from essential additions such as central heating, insulation, and putting floor boards and ceilings in the attic to create more bedrooms and another bathroom, they made no other changes – no fitted kitchen, no ensuite bathrooms – just an approximation to the style of the Sprotts. In this, they were helped enormously by Stephen Treasure and his craftsmen. His father had worked on the house for the Richardsons, and Stephen himself knows every inch of it from the roof to the cellars.

There was by this time a serious problem created by large vehicles crashing into the arch, on average about once a month. Drivers of lorries, horse-boxes and camper-vans regularly misjudged the height and width of the space under the building, and local 'boy-racers' saw it as a challenge to drive through as fast as possible. This resulted in considerable damage to the structure, as well as being a danger to pedestrians walking through the arch. Matters came to a head on 7th July 2005, when a small truck, with a cherry-picker crane on top, raced up Lower Broad Street and crashed into a beam at the north end of the arch, pulling several other beams out of their sockets. The arch was closed for five months until repairs had been made,

68. THE ENTRANCE HALL AT THE BROAD GATE TODAY

but then reopened with no further protection for the building in place. Only three years later did Shropshire Council finally devise a scheme for large wooden bollards at each end of the arch, and new paving to suggest shared space with pedestrians. On the whole, this has worked extremely well.

69. A LADY GIVES INSTRUCTIONS TO HER COOK
An illustration from Hannah Glasse's Art of Cookery made Plain and Easy, *first published 1747*

− 12 −

THE SERVANTS

The families who owned or leased the Broad Gate were not the only people living in the house. The way of life led by the Steads, the Sprotts, the Kinnersleys and the Lloyds could not have been sustained without the labour of live-in servants. In the eighteenth and nineteenth centuries, and for much of the twentieth, coal fires were essential to keep the house warm, grates needed to be swept and fires kept going, and the dust generated in almost every room meant that there was a constant process of cleaning. As more possessions were acquired by the family, so more articles and utensils needed attention. By the eighteenth century the role of a wife in a middle-class or professional household had become much less hands-on and she was more of a supervisor or manager of others. She did a good deal of needlework and, in many households, made shirts for the menfolk, but her social status required that she should not get her own hands dirty with cooking, cleaning or the immediate supervision of her children. Like Goldilocks, she had no longer to wash dishes nor yet feed the swine.

Ludlow is fortunate in that records of complete households paying taxes or rates in the eighteenth and early nineteenth centuries survive in the Poll Tax registers and in the Easter books, which give the annual rates paid to St Laurence's. The earliest servants we learn of are John Beech and Elizabeth

Woodall, servants of John Stead and his wife, Priscilla in 1689. John Beech was a medical apprentice to Dr Stead. We also know something of those who served the Sprott womenfolk. Anne Sprott, née Lockier, who, after her husband's death in 1663, had moved into Ludlow with her children at 8-9 Mill Street, had as many as six servants, which was a large household for a widow. By 1726 her daughter-in-law, Joyce Sprott, herself a widow, had one manservant and one maid when she moved her family into the Broad Gate. In 1729 she had a man and two maidservants. The Easter books give the numbers of servants but not their names. However, Elinor Addams and Margaret Wilmott, witnessed Joyce's will in 1731, and we know that Elinor, at least, was her servant, because, along with Sarah Haughton and Thomas Yapp, she was described as such when witnessing the will of Joyce Sprott's sister-in-law, Isabella. All three must have lived at the Broad Gate. Thomas Yapp had also witnessed the will of Dorothy Sprott, another sister-in-law, in 1728.

After his mother's death in 1732, Samuel Sprott lived alone at the Broad Gate, first with a maid and a manservant, and then with one manservant until his marriage. Thereafter, Samuel and his wife kept a man and two maidservants. Among the men and women who served them, we know that Richard Kendrick was left money for an apprenticeship in his master's will, and in 1756 Mary Morgan, 'servant to Dr Samuel Sprott', saw Elizabeth Butler stealing coals from the cellar.[152] After Samuel Sprott's death in 1760, his widow continued to employ a man and two maidservants. In 1763 one of her sisters-in-law was living with her with her own maid and this arrangement continued until Mary's death in 1772. There is a gap in the Easter Books between 1771 and 1785, so we do not know how many servants were kept by the tenants, Captain Poole, and then Mrs Congreve, though when Mrs Congreve lived elsewhere in Broad Street, she had two servants.

In 1785 James Kinnersley was living at the Broad Gate with his wife, a man and three maids. They had a man and two maids in 1787, when his wife's mother, Mrs Pardoe, was living with them with her own maid. By 1802, Lucy Kinnersley, now a widow, like Mary Sprott before her, still kept a man and two maids. Meanwhile, Henry Lloyd, who had arrived in Ludlow a few years earlier, and was living at St Leonard's House, Linney, kept four maids, no doubt to help with his large family. When he moved as a widower into the Broad Gate in 1816, his sister kept house for him, but he still had four maids. This continued when he married again a few years later, but in 1821 one of the maids had been replaced by a man, and Henry may well have had a groom before this, living elsewhere.

At the time of the earliest Census, 1841, John Lloyd had inherited the lease of the Broad Gate and was living there with his wife, Charlotte. They had no children, but they kept two maids, whose names and ages are given as Elizabeth Russell aged 32, and Esther Meredith aged 26. They also had a manservant, Walter Smith, who is described as 'mace-bearer', though this was presumably his secondary occupation.

In the census for 1851 the function of each servant is included as well as their ages. Fanny Tomkins aged 21, was the cook, Harriet Pearce aged 21, was the housemaid, and George Hodnet, aged 27, the groom. By 1861 John Lloyd had remarried and had three children. The servants are recorded as Nathaniel Lea aged 36, groom, Fanny Tomkins aged 30, cook, and Harriet Swain aged 22, housemaid. There is also a sixteen-year-old, Fanny Hall, who is described as an occasional nurse. This suggests either that she looked after all the children or that one of them in particular needed special attention. The latter possibility is borne out rather poignantly in 1871, when one of the servants, Mary Anne Lewis, is described as a 'nurse'. Although only eighteen, it was she who witnessed the death of the eldest son, John Charles on 27th November 1871. By this time, Fanny Lloyd was a widow with seven children, and two servants besides Mary Anne: Elizabeth Price aged 22, cook, and Elizabeth Wheeler aged 18, housemaid. She still had a manservant, Edmund Snowyell aged 31, who is described as gardener/

groom, but by 1881 she had either dispensed with him or he was living in the cottage in Silk Mill Lane. With five children still at home, she was served by Fanny Maund, cook, Mary Griffiths, parlourmaid, and Mary Millichamp, who was both house and laundry-maid. We have no record of the household in the 1891 census, as Fanny and her son George were away from home at Dursley in Gloucestershire, but in 1901 she was living at the Broad Gate with her spinster daughter, Effie, and three servants, Emily Jane Morris aged 20, cook, Margaret Morris aged 18, parlourmaid, and Mary Teague aged 13, housemaid.

We know from advertisements in the *Wellington Journal* that Fanny was having trouble between 1891 and 1908 in keeping up a full complement of household servants. Girls could work in factories or shops and many were now emigrating to the colonies in search of a better life. It was already the beginning of what became known as 'the servant problem'. In 1891 Fanny was advertising for a general servant:

Wanted thorough General, good plain cooking. Churchwoman, good references, two other servants.

It is clear that a general servant was expected to turn her hand to other things besides cooking. In 1894 Fanny wanted a second housemaid 'immediately' with a 'good character'. In 1896 and 1898 she was still wanting a good 'General or Plain Cook'. In October 1899 she was advertising again for 'two respectable girls … house-parlourmaid and housemaid, cook kept, some washing,' and then again in December for a 'housemaid (young) wanted, some washing, cook and parlourmaid kept'. In 1900 she wanted a house-parlourmaid again. She almost always asked for a 'churchwoman' and for good references. In January 1908 she advertised for 'a Cook-general (about 25), good wages to suitable servant, house-parlourmaid kept, gardener outdoors. Churchwoman, references'. She was careful to point out the number of servants she kept, to suggest the status of the household.

Many families further down the social scale kept a maid-of-all-work who would have to do everything.

The *Wellington Journal* was clearly a good paper in which to find servants, as it also carried advertisements for 'Situations Wanted' from the servants themselves. One of these, in July 1891, came from a servant at the Broad Gate:

> *Wanted. A situation as Working-house-keeper, where a servant is kept; understands baking and dairy; country preferred. Address D. Skennett, the Broad Gate, Ludlow.*

Perhaps she found Ludlow too urban or perhaps Fanny was a hard taskmaster who failed to keep her servants. Fanny's youngest son, Stanley, had married in 1900. He and his wife were living at Whitton House outside Ludlow with Mary Combi, cook, Ada Baker, housemaid, and a gardener, William Davies.

Ten years later, in 1911, when Fanny was 81 and Ethel 51, they were reduced to two servants in the house: Elizabeth Mary Ravenshill aged 20, the cook, and Elizabeth Jane Tomkinson aged 24, the housemaid. William Bayfield, the gardener, was a widower living with his two daughters in Broadgate Cottage. At Whitton House, Stanley and his wife, Amy, now had three children and employed a cook, Winifred Mary Bassett aged 29, a housemaid, Caroline Hughes aged 19, and a nurse for the children, Evelyn Mary Lloyd aged 19. After Fanny's death in 1915, Stanley's mother-in-law and sister-in-law were living at the Broad Gate, but we have no record of their servants.

The censuses for 1921 onwards have not yet been published, so it is not easy to know who worked at the Broad Gate after Stanley and his family moved into the house in 1920, but there was certainly still a cook at the house before the Second World War. Her son, who supplied this information, did not say whether she lived in or not, but in the letter of 1976, looking back at

70. TWO OF THE GIRLS WHO WORKED FOR STANLEY LLOYD'S FAMILY
photographed some time between 1920 and 1940. On the right, Hilda Preece, housemaid, with
Dick, the dog, and on the left, 'Baden-Powell' Preece, cook, with Toby, the cat

the time when the Lloyds still lived in the house, Mary Lloyd refers to maids in the kitchen and 'our two servants' bedrooms' on the top front level of the house. These may be the two servants who appear in a photograph owned by the Lloyd family which shows two girls in caps and aprons sitting on the lawn playing with the family cat and dog. One is labelled 'Hilda Preece, housemaid'; the other has the bizarre name of 'Baden Powell Preece, cook'. The cottage in Silk Mill Lane may still have been used for a gardener. When the Richardsons arrived in 1946 after the war had ended, they employed Bella Collier to work as a general help, but the era of the live-in servant had ended. The present owners were fortunate enough to inherit Bella when they first arrived. Since Bella's retirement, two good friends, Rowena Streatfield and occasionally her husband, Mark, have given invaluable assistance with the maintenance of the house.

What is noticeable about the female servants in the more distant past is that, apart from Elizabeth Russell, who was thirty-two in 1841, all the maids were in their teens or early twenties, and only one of them, Fanny Tomkins, seems to have stayed longer than ten years. This is presumably because most of them had to leave when they married and could no longer live in, though older married women living at home might come to work at the house for a specific reason such as sewing or laundry, or doing the 'rough' work. Married servants living in were not encouraged. Middle-aged cooks or housekeepers in larger houses might be given the courtesy title of 'Mrs', but employers did not want female servants who were distracted by spouses, children or a separate household. Those who stayed on as unmarried employees were often valued and rewarded, as can be seen from their employers' wills.

Young girls from workhouses or orphanages or straight from school as young as twelve or thirteen were often taken into service. In Daniel Defoe's novel of 1722, Moll Flanders, an orphan, is determined to avoid this, but in 1901 Mary Jane Teague, who may also have been an orphan, was at the age of thirteen working as a housemaid for Fanny Lloyd. When Anna Maria Fay paid a visit to a school overseen by Lady Harriet Clive in the old gatehouse at Bromfield, she found that 'when the girls are fourteen or fifteen, they go out to service in Ludlow or the neighbourhood, and if they do well, Lady Harriet recommends them whenever she can'.[153] Flora Thompson in *Lark Rise to Candleford,* writing about the early twentieth century, says that, at ten or eleven, after school, the village girls spent a year at home helping with the younger children, then were placed for a year in the households of tradesmen, grooms or schoolmasters, until they had learnt basic skills and were strong enough for 'gentlemen's service'.[154] Carola Oman in *An Oxford*

Childhood (1976), describes how her mother around 1910 had 'a succession of morning girls from Sister Ellen's Orphanage, who came to learn the ways of a house'.[155] They worked their way up as scullery or kitchen maids, to become cooks and parlour maids while still quite young.

Most of the maids at the Broad Gate in the eighteenth and nineteenth centuries were country girls from the local villages. On the whole, servant girls and their families were glad when they found a place in service in a prosperous household. It was better than working in the fields or being a burden to their parents. In any case, improvements in agriculture meant that girls had to look to the towns for employment. For 'kept' servants, such a post provided shelter, security, regular meals and often better food than at home, a bed of their own and sometimes their clothing as well. They lacked the independence they might have had as factory workers, but there were few jobs of that kind in the Ludlow area. They might also have been taught valuable skills which they could apply in their own families after marriage, and they had a unique opportunity to observe intimately manners and customs different from their own. When they left service to marry and set up their own households, it was customary for the brides to provide most of the furniture for the house; Flora Thompson describes how they tried to find items like those in the grander houses they had left behind – 'parlour' chairs, cushions, curtains, Japanese fans, books and flowers:

> *The young woman laying her own simple dinner table with knives and forks only could have told just how many knives, forks, spoons and glasses were proper to each place at a dinner party and the order in which they should be placed … they had seen the world and knew how things were done.* [156]

At first the girls might have been paid a few pounds a year, all found. This meant board and lodging with tea, sugar and sometimes, beer. Upper servants would have been paid more, and, with increasing social entertaining in the eighteenth and nineteenth centuries, there were opportunities for 'vails' or tips from guests and some perks on the side, particularly for cooks. In 1861, a kitchen maid might have made £8 - £12, a housemaid £10 - £17, a cook £12 - £26, and a housekeeper £18 - £40, with her own room. Some employers gave generous presents and cast-off clothes. As we have seen, servants who stayed with their employers could be rewarded in their wills. In her will of 1722 Alice Dawes stated:

> *I give and bequeath unto my maid Mary Griffiths who hath lived with me many years my Bed and bolster, two blankets, Two pair of Hempen sheets, Half a dozen of Huckaback Napkins, five plates, all my wearing apparel and all other my Clothes of all sorts whatsoever and my Shifts and also my little Square Table all to be delivered within one month of my decease.*

Isabella Sprott, eight years later, left her servant, Dorothy Harries 'her bed with hangings, furniture and a pair of hempen and a pair of flaxen sheets, plus £10'. There was a condition to Anne Pryce's bequest of a sum of 'eight pounds and a handsome suit of mourning to Anne Marston' and 'a handsome suit of mourning and a year's wages to Elizabeth Mill', both of them her servants. They only inherited if they were still in her service at the time of her death, and the same condition applied in 1915, when Fanny Lloyd left in her will twenty pounds free of duty 'to my servant William Bayfield, if he shall be in my service or working at the Broad Gate in the service of my family at the time of my decease'. Her daughter, Ethel, who had a maid, Agnes Deane, as late as 1940, left her 'the sum of sixty Pounds free of duty if she shall be in my service at the time of my death'. Servants in Ludlow were even occasionally left property or leases. In 1753, Richard Brown, attorney, left 40 Mill Street to his servant, Mary Jones. Selina Jones, who worked for Eliza Edwards, a spinster, at 4 Brand Lane, was left the lease of the house for her lifetime when Eliza died in 1846. The relationship between employer and maid could be a very close and friendly one, and it was a compliment to a master or mistress to say that a servant had grown old in their service.

But it was still a hard life. There was no job security and many servants had no home of their own to which they could go if they were out of work. If their employers died and they were too old to find new work, they very often ended up in the workhouse. At the Broad Gate the maids slept in unheated rooms, and in some households candles were forbidden for fear of fire. Hours of work were very long and time off very limited. The girls were allowed to admit their friends, but employers were afraid of potential burglars. 'Followers' were frowned on, so it is hard to see when they could do their courting; unwanted pregnancies usually led to dismissal. According to Flora Thompson, 'courtships were mostly conducted by letter'.[157] The young people hardly saw each other, apart from one fortnight at home in the summer. Servants might accompany their employers to church or on visits or to social functions, but it is probably significant that in October 1786 the Corporation banned servants from entering the Ball Room at the Market Hall, though the Bailiffs provided rooms for male servants at the public houses nearby. In earlier times, in a more paternalistic system, servants had been more integrated into the household (the word 'family' included the servants). They might have been poor, dependent relatives, and their work often entailed more than housework, especially on farms or in shops. Apprentices lived in, and ate with the family. But this was changing. Servants became increasingly distant from their employers. A system of bells on wires leading to the servants' quarters meant that they no longer had to be within calling distance or to sleep in truckle beds near their master or mistress. House servants were now much more likely to be women, as they were cheaper to employ, and the work became more specialized.

As the kitchen became the fixed centre for food production, so the cook had a full-time job, rising early to light the kitchen fire, and being responsible for cleaning and maintaining everything in the kitchen, as well as preparing all the food for the family's three large meals a day and feeding the other servants. The old hanging cauldrons of the past had been replaced with saucepans and skillets, often of copper which needed extra cleaning and polishing. In larger households the cook might have had a kitchen maid, though not at the Broad Gate. At the same time she would be expected to help with jobs that needed extra hands such as making beds or when the house had visitors.

The responsibilities of the parlourmaid included everything to do with the 'front of house' rooms, as well as answering bells and receiving visitors. The housemaid did everything else, including carrying coal and water and emptying the slops from washing bowls and chamber pots. Far more housework than is required nowadays was necessary in the days when carpets had to be swept by hand, grates blackened, steps whitened and fires attended to. One maid at the Broad Gate in 1881, Mary Millichamp, is described also as a laundry maid, an onerous job in a house where quantities of valuable sheets and table-linen would need to be washed as well as clothes, and where everything had covers or dust-sheets. For centuries, pure white linen and lace had been an indication of class. Often the laundry was done by women from outside who came every few weeks, but Fanny's advertisements in the *Wellington Journal* sometimes specify 'some washing'. It is possible that the brewery vats in the Broad Gate cellar may have been used also for the laundry, though the details of the house sale in 1813 mention a laundry on the same floor as the bedrooms, possibly the room which is now a bathroom. Sometimes ladies, like Lucy Kinnersley's mother, would have their own maids, who would have looked after their mistress's clothes and her hair.

By the nineteenth century, specialization had been taken to its limit. Mrs Beeton's advice to middle-class households is probably a counsel of perfection, but in her *Everyday Cookery and Housekeeping Book* (1865), the duties of the cook and the housemaid are clearly differentiated. For instance, the housemaid cleaned the ladies' shoes, while the cook cleaned those of the gentlemen. A rigid daily and weekly timetable of constant cleaning was to be adhered to. Duties were strictly defined and hardly a minute of the day was not accounted for. As we have seen with Fanny Lloyd's difficulties, by the 1890s it was already becoming hard to attract girls away from other occupations. 'Girls prefer machine toil to service with persons grown rich by machinery', as Frances McLaughlin put it in *The National Review* in 1891, but as she went on to say, 'Domestic service must go on. We can't cook our own dinners and keep our sumptuous houses clean'.[158]

The Broad Gate had no 'servants' hall', but in their rare moments of leisure, the maids could perhaps retreat to the kitchen, which was often a warm social centre where activities other than cooking, like sewing or childcare, might take place, though the windows were very often left wide open, if nineteenth and early twentieth-century photographs are anything to go by. Throughout this period, and probably until central heating became universal, there seems to have been a great belief in the value of fresh air. There was, therefore, a need for ventilation and open windows. In a photograph of the southern side of the house a group of happy faces appears at the open kitchen window. In one of her letters Mary Lloyd suggests that the maids used to let their boyfriends in through the windows, 'though it was always supposed to be forbidden'. It is hard to see how this could be done without a very long ladder.

Apart from the parlourmaid, the other female servants were meant to be more or less invisible, with their own back stairs from cellar to attic. Retaining a visible manservant, however, was a sign of status. In 1777, to raise money for the American War, a tax was imposed by Lord North on luxuries such as silver, carriages and men servants, so to employ one showed a certain level of prosperity. In a grand house, such a servant might have been a footman or a butler, but in a house like the Broad Gate he would probably have had several functions, gardener, groom, coachman, and valet. Most houses tried to keep male and female staff strictly segregated, but this was not always possible. After James Kinnersley's time, however, the cottage in Silk Mill Lane, next to the stables, was available for a gardener or groom to live in. We know that John Lloyd kept a groom. Both he and his father, Henry, and Samuel Sprott before them, had paid rent for fields nearby to pasture their horses, and the Broad Gate stables had room for two horses and a carriage, though Samuel Sprott's male servant, Richard Kendrick, was probably also his medical assistant, to whom he left £10 in his will for an apprenticeship. Some male servants had occupations beyond the household, as in the case of William Smith, the mace-bearer, or managed to save enough in 'vails' or tips to leave service altogether and start their own business. The *Hereford Journal* for 10th December 1794 has an advertisement from Thomas Bowen:

Angel Inn, Ludlow
Thomas Bowen
for several years servant to Mr Kinnersley
Begs leave to inform the Public that he opens the above inn at Christmas. T. Bowen hopes by his assiduity and attentions as well as a choice selection of WINES, LIQUORS, and every other Article necessary for the comfortable accommodation of the Public, to prove to those who shall honour him with their patronage how much it will be his constant endeavour to render his House worthy their support.

Finally, the other inhabitants of the house might be said to be the birds – the jackdaws who are always with us, and who clearly regard the house as their own, chattering companionably in the arrow-slit behind the Aga and occasionally falling down a chimney; and the swifts, who return every Spring to the eaves under the bathroom roof – alas, in fewer numbers each year. These days, pigeons proliferate and the robins and blackbirds are more elusive, but a sparrowhawk has been helping to keep down the pigeons, and a rare hobby has been seen flying across the valley. They all give a sense of timelessness to a building that has existed for well over eight hundred years.

71. THE GARDEN FRONT OF THE HOUSE

CONCLUSION

In many ways the Broad Gate is a unique building. There are other medieval town gates surviving in England, many with rooms above them, but not one with such a large residence built on to substantial medieval foundations, with a garden running along the top of the town wall. The Broad Gate's Georgian interior has also survived largely untouched, with few insensitive additions or alterations. Even the stable remains as it was when the last horse or pony left. It is a very unusual house.

On the other hand, the lives of the people who lived there are typical of those of professional families, doctors, bankers, lawyers, in any English town throughout the last four hundred years. There are the usual aspirations and ambitions of those with pride in their lineage, seeking higher status, and greater wealth through the acquisition of land and property, as well as influence in the town. There are instances of disappointing sons and heirs – white hopes turning into black sheep – or lines coming to an end for lack of a male heir. Several wives died exhausted by childbirth, but some of the women seem to have exerted a strong influence on the house, from the forceful and independent Sprott women to the long reign of Fanny Lloyd through the nineteenth and early twentieth centuries, and the single ownership of Annie Richardson after the Second World War. There was frequently a superfluity of spinster daughters, widows and widowers, and a fair number of premature deaths and sudden disasters.

At any time a country estate was always more important than its individual owner; the land gave income and status, and it could be associated strongly with the family over many generations. A town house was more of a temporary convenience. But the Broad Gate, a miniature country estate, has been lived in by few families for long periods, particularly by the Lloyds for a hundred and thirty-two years, and it is a house to which they have become seriously attached. They will have enjoyed the views of country fields from the south-facing kitchen windows, and Clee Hill, that 'vast mountain', to the east, changing in all seasons, sometimes with its head in the clouds, sometimes capped with snow like a little Alp. They will have seen everything going on in both Broad Street and Lower Broad Street, and from the hall windows will have shared the view of the Buttercross and the church tower, off-centre as it appears in Samuel Scott's painting. In the garden they will have heard sheep bleating from the farm beyond Whitcliffe, and been aware of the constant sound of the river Teme rushing over its weirs and its rocky bed to join the Severn. It is a magical house and, after the Steads, no family has left it willingly. They have remained in it for as long as they were able, and, unusually perhaps, have not sought to alter its essential character. The result is what John Newman, in the Pevsner Shropshire volume, describes as 'an extremely rare survival'.[159]

REFERENCES

NOTE ON THE REFERENCES

A good deal of the information about the house and its occupants is contained in the writings of the late David Lloyd (1935-2009), including his University of Wolverhampton Ph. D. thesis, his many books on Ludlow, and his working papers now in the possession of the Ludlow Historical Research Group. For the Lloyd family (not related to David) I have had access to the notes for a family history compiled by Michael Lloyd (1928-2003), material in the Weobley Museum Collection, and many facts and illustrations provided by present members of the family.

In addition to standard biographical sources such as parish records, wills, death certificates, census returns, trade directories and local newspapers, use has been made of poll tax, land tax, window tax and rate book returns for Ludlow to be found in Shropshire Archives. All of these are easily accessible and I have not usually given references for them. Ludlow Corporation Minutes contain records of leases and administrative orders for Ludlow, and the Easter books for St Laurence's Church give details of individual households. The deeds of the Broad Gate, dating from 1751 onwards, and other legal documents in my possession, have also provided valuable information.

ABBREVIATIONS

BL British Library
CPR *Calendar of Patent Rolls*
SA LB Ludlow Borough Records, in Shropshire Archives
LCM Ludlow Corporation Minutes, in Shropshire
LHRG Ludlow Historical Research Group
LPL Lambeth Palace Library
SA Shropshire Archives
TNA The National Archives

Unless otherwise stated, the place of publication is London.

INTRODUCTION

1. C. J. Train, *The Walls and Gates of Ludlow: their Origins and Early Days* (Ludlow, 1999), p. 2, n. 48; Neil Guy, 'Broad Gate, Ludlow: James of St George beyond North Wales?', *Castles: History, Archaeology, Landscape Architecture and Symbolism, Essays in honour of Derek Renn* (Daventry 2018).

2. BL, MS Cotton Nero, IV iv. fol. 48v (Llandaff Chronicle).

3. Nikolaus Pevsner, *The Buildings of England: Shropshire* (Harmondsworth, 1958), p. 187.

4. John Leland, *The Itinerary of John Leland in or about the year 1535*, ed. Lucy Toulmin Smith (1964), vol. 2, p. 76.

5. SA 356/391 (2nd August 1692).

6. *CPR Henry III, 1216-1225*, pp. 238-239.

7. For details of goods, and tolls levied on them, see Train, *Walls and Gates of Ludlow*, appendices 2 and 4.

8. TNA, SC 8/327/E859.

9. SA LB/8/1/7-12.

10. Arnold Taylor, *Conwy Castle and Town Walls* (4th edn. Cardiff, 1998), p. 5.

REFERENCES

11.   SA LB/8/1/6.

12.   Hilary L. Turner, *Town Defences in England and Wales* (1971), pp. 87-90.

13.   Henry T. Weyman, *Ludlow in Bye-Gone Days* (Ludlow, 1913), p. 57.

14.   SA LB/8/1/57 and Weyman, *Ludlow in Bye-Gone Days*, p. 58.

15.   SA LB/8/1/54; LCM 16/8/1656.

16.   SA LB/8/1/7.

17.   SA LB/2/1/3; SA 356/400 (1482).

18.   SA LB/8/1/7-12.

19.   Thomas Churchyard, *The Worthines of Wales* (1587; 1776), p. 76.

20.   SA LB/4/1/62.

21.   SA 357/347B.

22.   LCM 5/9/1599.

23.   SA LB/2/1/1, pp. 33, 105b.

24.   SA LB/4/3/1607.

25.   SA LB/2/1/1, p. 105.

26.   SA LB/4/3/120c. 1610; SA LB/4/1/405-6 1631: SA LB/4/1/516 1647.

27.   LCM 20/12/1634.

28.   SA 3365/551/59 (Shrewsbury Bailiffs' Accounts, 1608-9).

29.   *Records of Early English Drama: Shropshire*, ed. J. Alan B. Somerset (Toronto, 1944), vol. 1, pp. 301, 304.

30.   Caroline A. J. Skeel, *The Council in the Marches of Wales* (1904).

31.   Michael Faraday, *Ludlow 1085-1660* (Chichester, 1991), pp. 178-179.

32.   TNA C.5/591/16 (1647).

33.   SA LB/4/2/2, p. 44 (1672); SA LB/2/1/2, p. 278 (1672); LCM, p. 3 (1679).

34.   SA LB/4/3/180.

35.   SA LB/4/2/2, p. 157 (1688).

36.   SA LB/2/1/4, p. 37 (Jan. 1692/3)

CHAPTER 1

37. LCM 19/5/1756.

38. Letters on his behalf were signed by Hugh Chamberlain MD and Gideon Harvey MD; LPL, VX1A/10/252; LPL, VG1/6 f. 70; LPL, *Sancroft* 270.

39. SA LB/2/1/4 p. 37d; SA LB/27/1/1693.

40. LCM 1680, p. 18; SA LB/2/1/4; LCM 1690-1712, p. 66d.

41. SA LB/4/1/765 (1695).

42. Faraday, *Ludlow*, p. 179.

43. David Lloyd, *Property, Ownership and Improvement in Ludlow, a fashionable country town, 1660-1848* (University of Wolverhampton, Ph.D. thesis, 2005), pp. 243-69.

44. SA LB/2/1/3; LCM, 1680-90, p. 26.

45. TNA, C.8/485/36 (1708).

46. TNA, IR 5, fol. 98.

47. *Transactions between John Stead and his son Edward, and Samuel Waring Gent. Of Ludlow in the other party, 1729,* document in the possession of LHRG.

48. *Alumni Oxonienses 1500-1714,* comp. Joseph Foster (Oxford, 1891-92), vol. 4, p. 1415.

49. *The Warden's Punishment Book of All Souls College 1601-1850,* ed. Scott Mandelbrote and John H. R. Davis (Oxford Historical Society, 2013), pp. 339-340.

50. Charles Trice Martin, *The Archives in the Muniment Room of All Souls College* (Oxford 1877), pp. 355-380.

51. *Remarks and Collections of Thomas Hearne,* ed. Charles E. Doble *et al.* (Oxford Historical Society, 1885-1892), vol. 6, p. 236.

52. A full account of these events is to be found in Jeffrey R. Wigelsworth, *All Souls College Oxford in the Early Eighteenth Century: Piety, Political Imposition, and the Legacy of the Glorious Revolution* (Leiden, 2018), chap. 5.

53. Juanita G. L. Burnby, *A Study of the English Apothecary 1660-1760* (*Medical History,* Supplement no. 3, 1983), p. 12.

54. SA LB/4/3/393.

55. LCM 16/12/1724; LCM 22/8/1732.

56. LCM 13/10/1741.

57. SA LB/4/3/403; LCM 20/7/1725.

CHAPTER 2

58. John Newman and Nikolaus Pevsner, *Buildings of England: Shropshire* (2006), p. 133.

59. SA LB/2/1/5, p. 111.

60. David Lloyd, *Broad Street*, (Birmingham, 1979); Lloyd, 'Property, Ownership and Improvement'.

61. TNA, E134/19/Geo.2/Mich.3.

62. TNA, C12/263/45.

63. Susan Wright, 'Holding up Half the Sky', *Midland History*, 14 (1989), p. 53.

64. SA, 1987/3/8-9.

65. Julia Ionides, *Thomas Farnolls Pritchard, Architect and Inventor of Cast Iron Bridges* (Ludlow, 1999), p. 170.

66. LCM 22/10/1747; SA LB/4/3/930.

67. John Cornforth, *Early Georgian Interiors* (New Haven, CT, 2004), p. 13.

68. Ionides, *Thomas Farnolls Pritchard*, p. 44.

69. Newman, *Buildings of England: Shropshire*, p. 381.

70. Ionides, *Thomas Farnolls Pritchard*, pp. 45-46.

CHAPTER 3

71. Karen Banks, *The Ownership of Goods and Cultures of Consumption in Ludlow, Hereford and Tewkesbury, 1660-1760* (University of Birmingham, Ph.D. thesis, 2014), p. 97.

72. Foster, *Alumni Oxonienses*.

73. Burnby, *English Apothecary*, p. 8.

74. R. Campbell, *The London Tradesman*, (1747; Newton Abbot, 1969), p. 48.

75. Irvine Loudon, 'The Nature of Provincial Medical Practice in Eighteenth-century England', *Medical History*, 29 (1985).

76. *The Medical Consultation Letters of Dr William Cullen (1710-1790) at the Royal College of Physicians of Edinburgh*, www.cullenproject.ac.uk.

77. W.A.Felton, *A Description of the Town of Ludlow...an Informing and Useful Companion for the Residents and Visitants of this Ancient, Increasing and Elegant Town*, (Ludlow, 1812), pp. 90-91.

78. SA LB/3/1/974; LCM Nov. 1781.

79. This tablet was visible in St Giles Church, Ludford, in 1992, when it was recorded for the Shropshire Family History Society. Since then, with the renovation of the Fox Chapel, it has disappeared.

80. *Walpole Society*, vol. 32, p. 37.

81. SA LB/2/1/7, pp. 289-90; Broad Gate deeds, in possession of the author.

CHAPTER 4

82. *Passages from the Diaries of Mrs Lybbe Powys of Hardwick House Oxon, AD 1756-1808*, ed. Emily J. Climenson (1899), pp. 127-139.

83. Felton, *Description of the Town of Ludlow*, p. 122; *Thomas Wright, The History and Antiquities of the Town of Ludlow and its Ancient Castle* (Ludlow, 1826), pp. 210-211.

84. *Daniel Defoe, A Tour thro' the Island of Great Britain, 1724-6*, ed. G. D. H. Cole (1927), vol. 2, pp. 446-7.

85. Charles Burlington, *The Modern Universal British Traveller* (1779), p. 135.

86. Philip Luckombe, *The Beauties of England* (1764), p. 291.

87. *Diaries of Mrs Lybbe Powys*, p. 129.

88. *Diaries of Mrs Lybbe Powys*, p. 137.

89. John Macky, *Journey through England* (1722), vol.2, p. 41.

90. *Diaries of Mrs Lybbe Powys*, p. 137.

91. Carola Oman, *Ayot Rectory: a Family Memoir* (1965), p. 28.

92. *Diaries of Mrs Lybbe Powys*, p. 134.

93. Peter Barfoot and John Wilks, *The Universal British Directory* (1793-4), vol. 3, p. 28.

94. David Lloyd, *The Concise History of Ludlow* (Ludlow, 1999), p. 110.

95. Lloyd, *Concise History*, p. 110.

96. Oman, *Ayot Rectory*, p. 25.

97. Edward Gill, *Nelson and the Hamilton Tours* (Monmouth, 1987), p. 66.

98. Felton, *A Description of Ludlow*, p. 25.

99. Oman, *Ayot Rectory*, p. 46.

CHAPTER 5

100. Letters to Ludlow lawyers in the possession of LHRG.

101. LCM 28/10/1806.

102. Campbell, *The London Tradesman*, p. 80.

103. I am most grateful for sharing their knowledge of local canals to Dr David Slater, and to Bryan Heatley, whose article 'How a Canal almost came to Ludlow' appeared in *Ludlow Heritage News* (Winter, 1997).

104. Joseph Bullock, *The Beauties of Ludlow* (Ludlow, 1818).

105. The Broad Gate deeds, in the possession of the author.

CHAPTER 6

106. *Letters of Horace Walpole*, ed. Mrs Paget Toynbee (Oxford, 1903-1905), vol. 9, p. 78.

107. David Lloyd papers, LHRG.

108. *Life and Correspondence of Mrs Delaney*, ed. Lady Llanover (1816), vol. 1, p. 15.

109. *Diaries of Mrs Lybbe Powys*, p. 47.

110. Alan Brooks and Nikolaus Pevsner, *The Buildings of England: Worcestershire* (2007), p. 623.

111. Robert and James Adam, *The Works in Architecture* (1773-8), vol. 1, pp. 9-10.

112. Clive Edwards, *Turning Houses into Homes* (Aldershot, 2005), p. 22.

113. Pierre Bourdieu, *Distinction: a Social Critique of the Judgement of Taste*, trans. Richard Nice (Cambridge, MA, 1984), p. 76.

114. SA LB/4/3/539, 1731; SA LB/4/3/2017, 1731.

115. Peter Earle, *The Making of the English Middle Class* (1989), p. 298.

116. *The Diary of a Country Parson, the Reverend James Woodforde* ed. John Beresford (Oxford, 1931; 1968), vol. 4, p. 117.

117. *Diary of a Country Parson*, vol. 2, p. 91-92.

118. John Woodforde, *Georgian Houses for All* (1978), p. 50.

CHAPTER 7

119. A. E. W. Salt, *The Borough and Honour of Weobley* (Hereford, 1954). p. 46.

120. A copy of this drawing can be seen at Weobley Museum.

121. David Hey, *The Oxford Guide to Family History* (Oxford, 1993), p. 125.

122. Hey, *Guide to Family History*, p. 140.

123. James Macdonald and James Sinclair, *The History of Hereford Cattle* (1909), p. 117.

124. Newman, *Buildings of England: Shropshire*, p. 381.

CHAPTER 8

125. G. M. Young, *Portrait of an Age: Victorian England* (Oxford, 1977), p. 24.

126. Letters to Ludlow lawyers in the possession of LHRG.

127. The Packer scrapbook in David Lloyd's papers, LHRG.

128. For Francis Southern, see *Victorian Ludlow*, ed. LHRG (Trowbridge, 2004), pp. 188-193.

129. Christopher Train, *Crumbs from the Table of your Learning: letters to the Ludlow Historian, Thomas Wright* (Ludlow, 2006), pp. 13-21.

130. Letters to Ludlow lawyers, LHRG.

131. Campbell, *The London Tradesman*, p. 50.

132. J. C. Thackray, 'T. T. Lewis and Murchison's Silurian System', *Transactions of the Woolhope Naturalists Field Club Herefordshire,* 42 (1977), pp. 186 ff.; David Lloyd, *The History of Ludlow Museum, 1833-1983,* (Ludlow, 1983), pp. 4-5.

CHAPTER 9

133. SA LB/4/1/1764.

134. CM 11/12/1829.

135. Weyman, *Ludlow in Bye-Gone Days,* p. 57.

136. Anna Maria Fay, *Victorian Days in England: letters home by an American girl, 1851-2* (Ludlow, 2002), p. 86.

137. Katherine Plymley, *Journals,* vol. 35 (1795), quoted in Lloyd, 'Property, Ownership and Improvement', p. 54.

138. Felton, *Description of Ludlow,* pp. 138-140.

139. *A Land of Pure Delight: selections from the letters of Thomas Johnes of Hafod, Cardiganshire,* ed. Richard J. Moore-Colyer (1992), pp. 122 and 198.

140. Fay, *Victorian Days,* pp. 179-184.

141. Fay, *Victorian Days,* pp. 194 and 198.

142. Henry James, *Portraits of Places* (1883; 2001), pp. 243-4.

143. *Land of Pure Delight,* p. 13.

144. David Lloyd, *Country Grammar School* (n. pl., 1977), p. 115.

145. Lloyd, *Country Grammar School,* p. 122.

CHAPTER 10

146. Humphry Repton, *Fragments on the Theory and Practice of Landscape Gardening* (1816), cited in John Fowler and John Cornforth, *English Decoration in the Eighteenth Century* (1984), p. 75.

147. LCM 25/4/1757; LCM 6/5/1858.

148. Letter from David Lloyd to Mary Lloyd, in private possession.

149. Broad Gate deeds, in the possession of the author.

CHAPTER 11

150. SA 4924/1/42/11/1-2.

151. Letters from Mary Lloyd to David Lloyd, in private possession.

CHAPTER 12

152. SA LB/4/183/(QS).

153. Fay, *Victorian Days*, p. 121.

154. Flora Thompson, *Lark Rise to Candleford* (Oxford, 1939; 1954), p. 165.

155. Carola Oman, *An Oxford Childhood* (1976), p. 141.

156. Thompson, *Lark Rise*, p. 81.

157. Thompson, *Lark Rise*, p. 176.

158. Frances McLaughlin, 'The Problem of Domestic Service', *The National Review*, March 1891.

CONCLUSION

159. Newman, *The Buildings of England: Shropshire*, p. 381.

SELECT BIBLIOGRAPHY

Unless otherwise stated, all books are published in London.

Robert and James Adam, *The Works in Architecture* (1773-8)

Peter Barfoot and John Wilkes, *The Universal British Directory* (1793-4)

John Beresford, ed., *The Diary of a Country Parson, the Reverend James Woodforde* (Oxford, 1931; 1968)

Peter Borsay, *The English Urban Renaissance* (Oxford, 1989)

Peter Brears, *The Compleat Housekeeper* (Wakefield, 2000)

Alan Brooks and Nikolaus Pevsner, *The Buildings of England: Worcestershire* (2007)

Joseph Bullock, *The Beauties of Ludlow* (Ludlow, 1818)

Charles Burlington, *The Modern Universal British Traveller* (1779)

Juanita G. L. Burnby, *A Study of the English Apothecary* (*Medical History*, Supplement no. 3, 1983)

R. Campbell, *The London Tradesman* (1747; Whitstable, 1969)

Thomas Churchyard, *The Worthines of Wales* (1587; 1776)

Emily J. Climenson, *ed., Passages from the Diaries of Mrs Lybbe Powys of Hardwick House Oxon. AD 1756-1808* (1899)

John Cornforth, *Early Georgian Interiors* (New Haven CT, 2004)

Daniel Defoe, *A Tour thro' the Island of Great Britain, 1724-6* ed. G. D. H. Cole (1927)

Charles E. Doble et al., ed., *Remarks and Collections of Thomas Hearne* (Oxford Hist. Soc., 1885-1892)

Peter Earle, *The Making of the English Middle Class* (1989)

Clive Edwards, *Turning Houses into Homes* (Aldershot, 2005)

Michael Faraday, *Ludlow, 1085-1660* (Chichester, 1999)

Anna Maria Fay, *Victorian Days in England* (Ludlow, 2002)

W. A. Felton, *A Description of the Town of Ludlow* (Ludlow, 1812)

Joseph Foster, *Alumni Oxonienses* (Oxford, 1891-92)

John Fowler and John Cornforth, *English Decoration in the Eighteenth Century* (1984)

Edward Gill, *Nelson and the Hamiltons on Tour* (Gloucester, 1987)

Mark Girouard, *The English Town* (1990)

Neil Guy, 'Broad Gate, Ludlow; James of St George beyond North Wales?', *Castles: History, Archaeology, Landscape Architecture and Symbolism, Essays in honour of Derek Renn* (Daventry 2018)

Karen Harvey, 'Oeconomy and the Eighteenth-century House', *Journal of Architecture, Design and Domestic Space,* 11 (2014)

J. Jean Hecht, *The Domestic Servant Class in Eighteenth-century England* (1956)

David Hey, *The Oxford Guide to Family History* (Oxford, 1993)

Michelle Higgs, *Servants' Stories* (Barnsley, 2015)

Bridget Hill, *Servants* (Oxford, 1996)

Julia Ionides, *Thomas Farnolls Pritchard of Shrewsbury: Architect and Inventor of Iron Bridges* (Ludlow, 1999)

Henry James, *Portraits of Places* (1883; 2001)

Ben W. Johnson, *Digging in the Dark* (Barnsley, 2017)

Lady Llanover, ed., *The Autobiography and Correspondence of Mary Granville, Mrs Delaney* (1861-2; 1974)

David Lloyd, *Country Grammar School* (Ludlow, 1977)

SELECT BIBLIOGRAPHY

David Lloyd, *Broad Street* (Birmingham, 1979)

David Lloyd, *The History of Ludlow Museum* (Ludlow 1983)

David Lloyd and Peter Klein, *Ludlow, a Historic Town* (Chichester, 1984)

David Lloyd and Peter Klein, *Ludlow, an Historical Anthology* (Chichester, 1984)

David Lloyd, *The Concise History of Ludlow* (Ludlow, 1999)

Irvine Loudon, 'The Nature of Provincial Medical Practice in Eighteenth-century England', *Medical History*, 29 (1985)

Philip Luckombe, *The Beauties of England* (2nd edition, 1764)

Ludlow Historical Research Group, *Victorian Ludlow* (Ludlow 2004)

James MacDonald and James Sinclair, *The History of Hereford Cattle* (1909)

John Macky, *A Journey through England* (1722)

Frances McLaughlin, 'The Problem of Domestic Service', *The National Review*, (March 1891)

Scott Mandelbrote and John H. R. Davis, eds., *The Warden's Punishment Book of All Souls College* (Oxford Hist. Soc., 2013)

Charles Trice Martin, *The Archives in the Muniment Room of All Souls College* (Oxford, 1877)

Richard J. Moore-Colyer, ed., *A Land of Pure Delight: Selections from the Letters of Thomas Johnes of Hafod, Cardiganshire* (Llandysul,1992)

Craig Muldrew, *The Economy of Obligation* (Basingstoke, 1998)

A. J. Munby, *ed., Faithful Servants* (1891)

John Newman and Nikolaus Pevsner, *Buildings of England: Shropshire* (2006)

Carola Oman, *Ayot Rectory: a Family Memoir* (1965)

Carola Oman, *An Oxford Childhood* (1976)

Nikolaus Pevsner, *The Buildings of England: Shropshire* (Harmondsworth, 1958)

Wilfrid Prest, ed. *The Professions in Early Modern England* (Beckenham, 1987)

Phyllis M. Ray, *The Ashford Court Estate, 1600-1950* (Ludlow, 2017)

R. C. Richardson, *Household Servants in Early Modern England* (Manchester, 2010)

Robert Robson, *The Attorney in Eighteenth-century England* (Cambridge, 1959)

A. E. W. Salt, *The Borough and Honour of Weobley* (Hereford, 1954)

Pamela Sambrook and Peter Brears, *The Country House Kitchen* (Stroud, 1996)

Caroline, A. J. Skeel, *The Council in the Marches in Wales* (1904)

Lucy Toulmin Smith, ed., *The Itinerary of John Leland in or about the Year 1535* (1964)

J. Alan B. Somerset, ed., *Records of Early English Drama: Shropshire* (Toronto, 1994)

John Stobart and Mark Rothery, *Consumption and the Country House* (Oxford, 2016)

Dorothy Margaret Stuart, *The English Abigail* (1946)

John Styles and Amanda Vickery, ed., *Gender, Taste and Material Culture* (2006)

Arnold Taylor, *Conwy Castle and Town Walls* (Cardiff, 1998)

J. C. Thackray, 'T. T. Lewis and Murchison's Silurian System', *Transactions of the Woolhope Naturalists Field Club Herefordshire,* 42 (1977)

Flora Thompson, *Lark Rise to Candleford* (1945: 1954)

Peter Thornton, *Authentic Décor: Domestic Interior, 1620-1920* (1984)

C. J. Train, *The Walls and Gates of Ludlow: their Origins and Early Days* (Ludlow, 1999)

Christopher Train, *Crumbs from the Table of your Learning: letters to the Ludlow Historian, Thomas Wright* (Ludlow, 2006)

Mrs Paget Toynbee, ed., *The Letters of Horace Walpole* (Oxford, 1903-4)

Hilary L. Turner, *Town Defences in England and Wales* (1971)

Amanda Vickery, *Behind Closed Doors: At Home in Georgian England* (2009)

Henry Weyman, *Ludlow in Bye-Gone Days* (Ludlow, 1913)

Jeffrey R. Wigelsworth, *All Souls College in the Early Eighteenth Century: Piety, Political Imposition and the Legacy of the Glorious Revolution* (Leiden, 2018)

John Woodforde, *Georgian Houses for All* (1978)

Susan Wright, 'Holding up Half the Sky', *Midland History,* 14 (1989)

Thomas Wright, *The History and Antiquities of the Town of Ludlow and its Ancient Castle* (Ludlow, 1826)

G. M. Young, *Portrait of an Age: Victorian England,* ed. George Kitson Clark (1977)

SELECT BIBLIOGRAPHY

UNPUBLISHED THESES

Karen Egan-Banks, *The Domestic Interior and Material Culture of Ludlow 1700-1760*, (M.Phil thesis, Birmingham University, 2004)

Karen Egan-Banks, *The Ownership of Goods and Cultures of Consumption in Ludlow, Hereford and Tewkesbury, 1660-1670*, (D.Phil thesis, Wolverhampton University, 2014)

David Lloyd, *Property, Ownership and Improvement in Ludlow, a Fashionable Country Town, 1660-1848*, (D.Phil. thesis, Wolverhampton University, 2005)

THE BROAD GATE

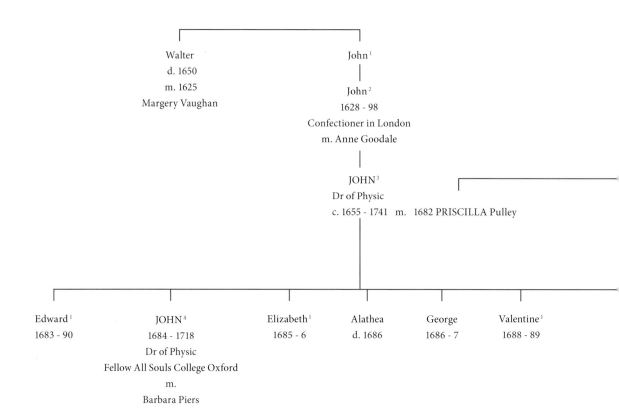

Walter
d. 1650
m. 1625
Margery Vaughan

John[1]

John[2]
1628 - 98
Confectioner in London
m. Anne Goodale

JOHN[3]
Dr of Physic
c. 1655 - 1741   m.   1682 PRISCILLA Pulley

Edward[1]
1683 - 90

JOHN[4]
1684 - 1718
Dr of Physic
Fellow All Souls College Oxford
m.
Barbara Piers

Elizabeth[1]
1685 - 6

Alathea
d. 1686

George
1686 - 7

Valentine[1]
1688 - 89

THE STEAD FAMILY TREE

Capital letters denote those who lived in the house

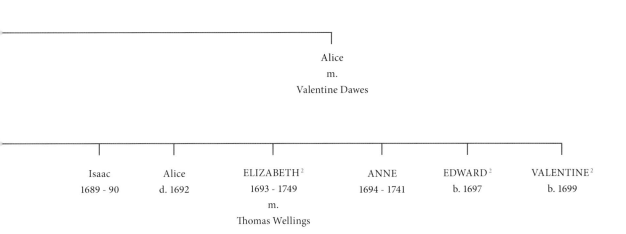

Alice
m.
Valentine Dawes

Isaac	Alice	ELIZABETH²	ANNE	EDWARD²	VALENTINE²
1689 - 90	d. 1692	1693 - 1749	1694 - 1741	b. 1697	b. 1699
		m.			
		Thomas Wellings			

The superscript numbers in all the family trees relate to the entries in the index
and indicate the successive individuals sharing the same Christian name.

THE BROAD GATE

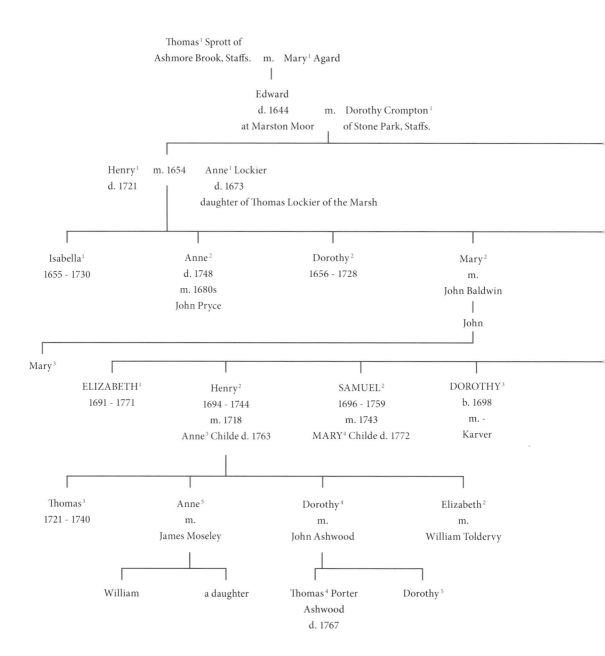

Thomas[1] Sprott of
Ashmore Brook, Staffs.   m.   Mary[1] Agard

Edward
d. 1644   m.   Dorothy Crompton[1]
at Marston Moor   of Stone Park, Staffs.

Henry[1]   m. 1654   Anne[1] Lockier
d. 1721   d. 1673
                        daughter of Thomas Lockier of the Marsh

Isabella[1]   Anne[2]   Dorothy[2]   Mary[2]
1655 - 1730   d. 1748   1656 - 1728   m.
                    m. 1680s   John Baldwin
                    John Pryce
                                                             John

Mary[3]

ELIZABETH[1]   Henry[2]   SAMUEL[2]   DOROTHY[3]
1691 - 1771   1694 - 1744   1696 - 1759   b. 1698
                    m. 1718   m. 1743   m. -
                    Anne[3] Childe d. 1763   MARY[4] Childe d. 1772   Karver

Thomas[3]   Anne[5]   Dorothy[4]   Elizabeth[2]
1721 - 1740   m.   m.   m.
                    James Moseley   John Ashwood   William Toldervy

                William   a daughter   Thomas[4] Porter   Dorothy[5]
                                         Ashwood
                                         d. 1767

236

THE SPROTT FAMILY TREE

Capital letters denote those who lived in the house

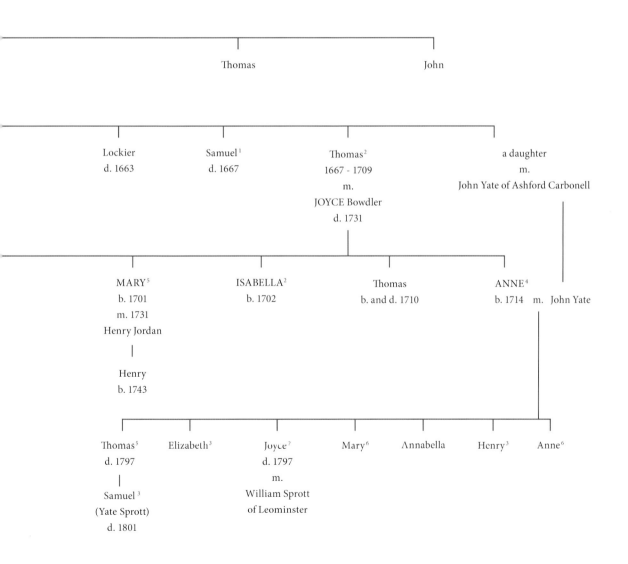

Thomas   John

Lockier
d. 1663

Samuel[1]
d. 1667

Thomas[2]
1667 - 1709
m.
JOYCE Bowdler
d. 1731

a daughter
m.
John Yate of Ashford Carbonell

MARY[5]
b. 1701
m. 1731
Henry Jordan

Henry
b. 1743

ISABELLA[2]
b. 1702

Thomas
b. and d. 1710

ANNE[4]
b. 1714 m. John Yate

Thomas[5]
d. 1797

Samuel[3]
(Yate Sprott)
d. 1801

Elizabeth[3]

Joyce[7]
d. 1797
m.
William Sprott
of Leominster

Mary[6]

Annabella

Henry[3]

Anne[6]

THE BROAD GATE

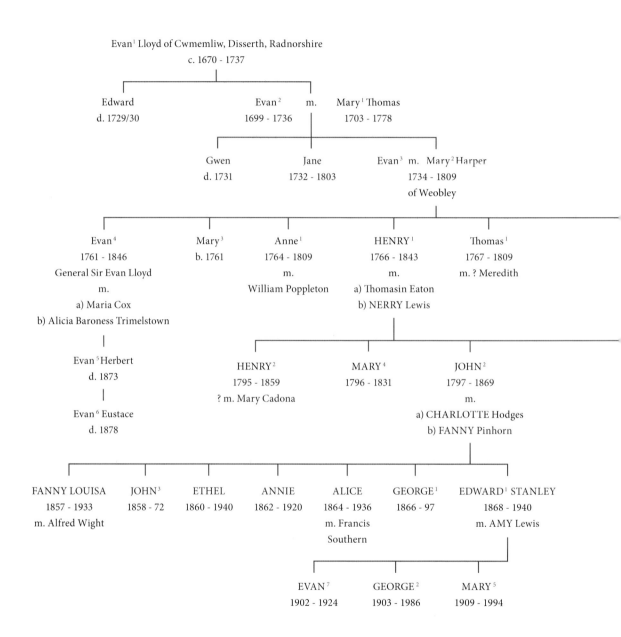

Evan¹ Lloyd of Cwmemliw, Disserth, Radnorshire
c. 1670 - 1737

Edward
d. 1729/30

Evan² m. Mary¹ Thomas
1699 - 1736   1703 - 1778

Gwen
d. 1731

Jane
1732 - 1803

Evan³ m. Mary² Harper
1734 - 1809
of Weobley

Evan⁴
1761 - 1846
General Sir Evan Lloyd
m.
a) Maria Cox
b) Alicia Baroness Trimelstown

Mary³
b. 1761

Anne¹
1764 - 1809
m.
William Poppleton

HENRY¹
1766 - 1843
m.
a) Thomasin Eaton
b) NERRY Lewis

Thomas¹
1767 - 1809
m. ? Meredith

Evan⁵ Herbert
d. 1873

HENRY²
1795 - 1859
? m. Mary Cadona

MARY⁴
1796 - 1831

JOHN²
1797 - 1869
m.
a) CHARLOTTE Hodges
b) FANNY Pinhorn

Evan⁶ Eustace
d. 1878

FANNY LOUISA
1857 - 1933
m. Alfred Wight

JOHN³
1858 - 72

ETHEL
1860 - 1940

ANNIE
1862 - 1920

ALICE
1864 - 1936
m. Francis
Southern

GEORGE¹
1866 - 97

EDWARD¹ STANLEY
1868 - 1940
m. AMY Lewis

EVAN⁷
1902 - 1924

GEORGE²
1903 - 1986

MARY⁵
1909 - 1994

THE LLOYD FAMILY TREE

Capital letters denote those who lived in the house

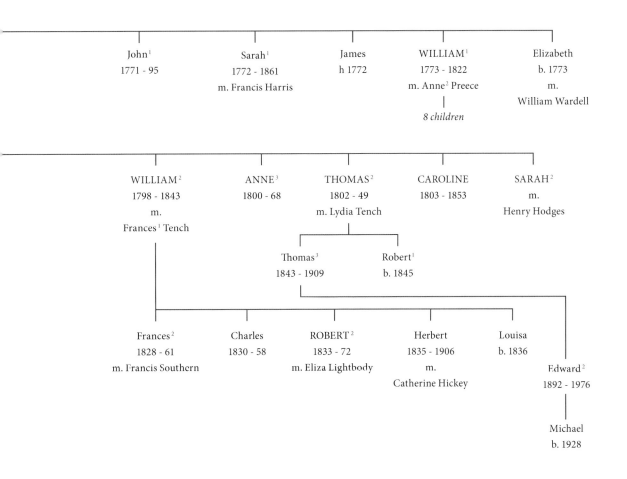

John[1] 1771 - 95	Sarah[1] 1772 - 1861 m. Francis Harris	James h 1772	WILLIAM[1] 1773 - 1822 m. Anne[2] Preece	Elizabeth b. 1773 m. William Wardell

8 children

WILLIAM[2] 1798 - 1843 m. Frances[1] Tench	ANNE[3] 1800 - 68	THOMAS[2] 1802 - 49 m. Lydia Tench	CAROLINE 1803 - 1853	SARAH[2] m. Henry Hodges

Thomas[3] 1843 - 1909   Robert[1] b. 1845

Frances[2] 1828 - 61 m. Francis Southern	Charles 1830 - 58	ROBERT[2] 1833 - 72 m. Eliza Lightbody	Herbert 1835 - 1906 m. Catherine Hickey	Louisa b. 1836

Edward[2] 1892 - 1976

Michael b. 1928

72. A DECORATIVE IRON GATE IN THE PRESENT BROAD GATE GARDEN

INDEX

...ower Garden lying below the B...
...and Wainwright and afterward...
...ast had been thrown and then...
...l whereon several Tenements or...
...ssuage or Tenement formerly of...
...ly in the possession of Samuel...
...and afterwards of the said...
...u Ground on the West the Four...
...d Messuage or Tenement lake...
...called the Broad Gate on the...
...Lloyd and William Lloyd...
...divided from the other part of...
...st mentioned Messuage or Te...
...years past thrown and then...
...el Sprott Esquire and afterwa...
...ssages buildings Gardens here...